PURPOSE, PASSION & PERFORMANCE

HOW SYSTEMS FOR LEADERSHIP, CULTURE & STRATEGY DRIVE THE 3Ps OF HIGH-PERFORMING ORGANISATIONS

STEPHANIE BOWN

Project management and text design by Publish Central
Cover design by Peter Reardon

Contents

Foreword

Imagine a world where everyone feels fulfilled and driven by purpose in the work they do. How much better would society be as a result?

As business leaders, it is our responsibility to create productive, inspiring workplaces. Spaces where people love what they do and are passionate about their purpose. When people love what they do, they bring their best game. It's not an effort; it just feels good.

Swisse, Australia's leading wellness brand, had an inspirational Founding partner and Managing Director in Michael Saba who was very much involved in driving it to where it was when I arrived. He was supported by his visionary business partner, Stephen Ring. Both gentlemen did the hard part starting up the business, laying foundations built on best product, brand focus and culture. It then required someone to create the foundation for its next stage of expansion. When I joined in 2005, I'd just come from Village Roadshow and knew what systems could do for a business. After a considered handover, I stepped in as CEO in 2008, and over the next 10 years, we grew Swisse from a $14 million business to a $750 million enterprise.

The key to our growth was making sure we brought on the right people who shared our cultural values and passion for wellness – and could build systems and structures. Yes, we faced challenges along the way. Revenue never stopped growing, but we had issues underlying profitability, which I attributed to systems not growing as fast as they could.

Stephanie Bown joined us in 2014 and was one of the key architects of the systems for culture, strategy and leadership, enabling another evolution of growth that helped take us from a $300 million to a $750 million operation. Swisse was in a great position to go well beyond a billion.

Steph helped us create a culture that made us clearly one of the best employers in this country, recognised by multiple Employer of Choice awards. We were the fastest growing business globally in our category for eight years straight – and that's just unheard of in a mature category.

Steph's role was central to making sure that we transitioned into being a global business, and I'd always loved talking about her role as being like our internal coach. Having someone focus purely on the performance of the business was revolutionary at the time. Elite athletes and great sporting clubs all have performance coaches. So, why wouldn't a business want to help their team become better at what they do?

I believe that a leader must live, breathe and believe the culture and the business strategy. Be obsessed, intoxicated by it to the point where they think about it all the time. High-performance cultures lead to outcomes where people feel recognised, rewarded and part of something that's satisfying. The great challenge of leadership is maintaining that balance and getting that right.

Savvy leaders use Business Plans to identify potential opportunities and avoid pitfalls but very few develop strategies for culture – even fewer have a communication plan that underpins it all. We regularly talk about delivering on budgets but how often do we talk about delivering on our Culture Plan and making sure that businesses are equally accountable to all those mechanisms we know are fundamental to creating success?

Systems spell things out. They're the oil that allows the engine to turn. They also provide a framework that facilitates company growth. I see lots of high-energy individuals who focus on early growth without having any real structure in place for long-term success.

You can't have performance without strategy, and this is particularly critical for businesses as they become larger. Unless there's a policy that binds people together and provides a reference point, a business will quickly lose direction and fail.

Responsible leaders are always thinking ahead to their next inflection point of the business. With *Purpose, Passion and Performance*, Steph gives you a box of tricks, a source of inspiration, which you can constantly draw upon to ensure you are always one step ahead. This equips CEOs, team leaders and C-level executives with the essential tools to steer their businesses in the right direction.

The difference between a high-performing business and a pedestrian one is culture. And, as Steph successfully demonstrates, systems are what's needed to build and maintain a positive, supercharged culture where people are focused on outcomes and rewarded for their efforts. Your business could be in any one of three modes – high growth, maintaining, or decline – and you may experience these over many cycles. To adapt, the business needs to have the right systems in place to regularly review who or what is managing culture and elevating performance.

What's particularly striking about this book is the amazing amount of wonderful ideas and contextual examples that give you a deep insight into why a system was successful. There are these nice little anecdotes of, 'Well, if you're in this situation, have you thought about this or that?' It's about finding the relevant systems and processes that work for you at the right time.

A kaleidoscope of wonderful ideas, *Purpose, Passion and Performance* is an easy read and moves at a pace that enables you to really think about each insight and its relevance to your business. The delivery is measured and considered, giving you the opportunity to implement learnings and integrate them into your existing practices.

Whether you are an aspiring or recently appointed CEO, or a seasoned veteran honing your skillset, this book will give you the tools to implement high-performance systems within your own organisation.

Radek Sali
Chairman of Light Warrior Group & Lightfolk Foundation
Former CEO of Swisse Wellness

Preface

When I was 15 years old, my Uncle Nick set me on a path that has led me to where I am today.

I was in year 10 and was about to choose my subjects for my final years of high school. I'd known early on that I was interested in psychology. But there were other careers I was drawn to (anthropology, osteopathy, psychiatry), and the decision felt big. And tinkering with people's minds is a big responsibility – what if I mess it up?! Secretly, what I was really questioning was whether I was even cut out for a career in psychology.

My dad suggested that I do a psychometric test with his cousin Nick – an organisational psychologist running a private practice.

Nick was tall and athletic. When he smiled, his whole face lit up. He had a big laugh. I grew up playing backyard cricket with his kids at Christmas parties in Warrandyte. I respected him. I wanted to impress him. In his office in Melbourne's CBD, he guided me through several psychometric tests to measure my intelligence, personality, preferences and learning styles.

Nick had these incredible blue eyes, and I felt like he was looking straight into my soul when he told me his conclusion: 'You'll make a great psychologist.'

Sweet relief charged through my system. I wasn't fooling myself. I *was* on the right track.

Then he presented me with two choices.

'All you need to do now is decide whether to work with sick people or well people.' He went on to explain that as a psychologist, you're either helping people get mentally well; or helping people achieve their best state. Again, I instinctively knew the answer. I wanted to work with well people, and I wanted to move them towards high performance.

Fast forward past three university degrees, accreditations in psychometric tools, almost a decade as a management consultant, a marriage, two children, and starting my own practice; I've culminated 10,000 hours working with leaders at every level, in every industry, in all kinds of businesses from start-ups to corporates, not for profits and government departments.

In my practice, I work with and talk daily with CEOs, founders, entrepreneurs and executives who are seeking help to make their businesses work better, their teams operate better, and their lives a little less hectic. They are juggling multiple balls. They are busy people. They are responsibility heavy and time poor. In short, they need me to cut to the chase.

I've written this book for these people.

I have two super strengths. One is listening. I use that one a lot when I'm working face to face with these people. The other is translating complex theory into simple how-to's – which is what I'm doing with this book. My goal is to:

1. show you how high-performance systems produce high-performing teams

2. give you the tools to implement high-performance systems within your own organisation.

Management theory, leadership theory and psychological research is all great stuff. It often tells us *why* we need to operate in certain ways, and *what* we need to do. But it doesn't tell us *how*.

This book aims to fast-track your leadership effectiveness by giving you just enough evidence to back up the theory, as well as the simple tools for putting best practice *into practice*.

Everything in this book I have implemented, honed and refined with real clients over many years. They have adopted these systems and processes as their own, trained newcomers in them, and given them their own language and life within the culture of their businesses.

My clients have been my teachers. Their experiences and stories have encouraged me to share this knowledge with a broader audience, in the hope that many more people will work in businesses that maximise human potential in the service of purposeful work.

***

My Uncle Nick died shortly after his 60th birthday. He had a heart attack. He and his beautiful wife, my Auntie Mal, were doing something as banal as watching a movie one Friday evening. Out of nowhere, Nick collapsed, and he wouldn't ever get up. The ambulance was called but there was nothing they could do. He died in the arms of his wife and daughter.

There aren't many days I don't think of Uncle Nick and thank him for the gift of confidence and inspiration he gave me that day when I was 15.

This book is for you, Nick. You're the standard I aspire to.

Introduction

How many of us wake up on any given workday and think to ourselves, *I hope I do a mediocre job today?* My guess is zero.

Nobody strives to be average. We all start with an intention to perform to our highest standard. To run our businesses, love our families, serve our customers, support our colleagues, and grow our communities in ways that are the expressions of our deepest values and beliefs. We aspire each day to show up as the best version of ourselves.

The reality, though, is that many of us are feeling overwhelmed in some areas of our lives and underwhelmed in others. We languish in apathy, frustrated by the repetitive and predictable aspects of our jobs and lives. Or we struggle in stress, overwhelmed by worry, competing priorities and multiple distractions. Under these conditions, it's very hard to 'show up as our best self'. We're doing well enough to just survive.

THE INCREASING PACE OF CHANGE

The pace of change has been ramping up since the emergence of digital technologies, and isn't showing signs of slowing anytime soon. We are living in what has been described as a 'VUCA' world. VUCA is an acronym introduced by the US Army War College to describe situations that are Volatile, Uncertain, Complex and Ambiguous. It was coined during the Cold War. It is now a shorthand way to recognise the cluster-f@*k we now find ourselves in (another useful US Army terminology).

The world was already struggling under the combined weight of rapid technological advancement, globalised economies, political instability and environmental crises.

Then came 2020.

Devastating bushfires in Australia wiped out 34 lives, 18.6 million hectares of agricultural land and forest, and over 5900 buildings (including 2779 homes). Widespread flooding added another $936 million of damage to the already fire-devastated state of NSW. And finally, the icing on the catastrophe cake: COVID-19. At the time of writing in September 2020, the coronavirus has killed almost one million people globally, sent sharemarkets around the world crashing at unprecedented rates, and put tens of millions of people into unemployment.

The events of 2020 have only added layers of complexity to the challenges we face as nations and a human race.

WE NEED ORGANISATIONS THAT ARE ADAPTIVE AND RESILIENT

To thrive in a VUCA world, we need organisations that are adaptive and resilient.

What we need now are strategies that build strength and adaptability in human beings, organisations, communities and whole societies. And the place where we need to build these capacities – the place where most populations of the world spend a third of their time – is at work.

> **Workplaces, and specifically leaders within workplaces, have the opportunity to effect positive and constructive change on a massive scale.**

The problems we face are so huge and so complex that governments cannot be left to deal with these issues alone. Change will take collaboration, innovation and clever thinking from the entire business community working to both influence and enact policy change.

If you are a CEO, founder, director or leader, you know you can't control external events. No one can know or control when the next pandemic hits. When the next natural disaster hits. When the government instigates taxes and incentives to protect our natural environment. All of these things *will* happen, and to pretend they won't is simply naïve and shortsighted.

If you're a business owner or leader, what you *can* influence is the way your organisation is set up to respond to these events. What you *can* do is create the conditions for performance in your business by focusing on the systems that connect, align and inspire your people.

This book is about how you can build a system of performance which creates the internal requisite variety to adapt to any market condition and weather any storm. It describes three key systems that enable high performance:

1. A leadership system.

2. A culture system.

3. A strategy system.

Systems create habits, which create results.

Leadership drives *purpose*, culture drives *passion*, and strategy drives *performance*. Together, the 3Ps – purpose, passion and performance – equal profit. And profit is the life-giving blood of the economy.

Without building systems for these three critical organising and aligning processes, you leave them up to chance. You put yourself, your team and your business at risk by relying on your old systems or pre-existing habits to sustain the performance of the business – systems and habits that may no longer be relevant in this new business environment.

Part I

The High-Performance System

'A handful of problems arise when you
spend too much time thinking about your goals
and not enough time designing your systems.'

James Clear, *Atomic Habits*

1

Understanding high performance

There's something beautiful about a team of people in their performance zone. Whether it's a game of elite football, an orchestra, a ballet, a band, chefs at service in a three-hat restaurant, or an emergency response team. It doesn't matter if that team is young or old, experienced or not, many or few. When individuals – each with unique personalities, quirks, fears, hopes and dreams – find formation and click into place to collectively and enthusiastically produce an exceptional result, it's nothing short of joyful.

> **These are high-performing teams; teams that effectively leverage collective capacity to achieve team synergy, where the whole is greater than the sum of the parts.**

In business, as in sport and the arts, to be a high-performing team it is a prerequisite to have high expectations. We can't be market leading unless we ask for exceptional, seek continuous improvement, drive continuous growth, and search for continuous innovation. This is the only way to attract and retain the best. This is why companies such as Google, Apple, 3M and Atlassian have talented people lining up to join them. People seek businesses where they see opportunities to learn, grow and improve. People want to be challenged. And they want to feel safe, valued and – above all – inspired.

My mentor and now great friend, the ex-Director of People & Culture at Swisse Wellness, Catherine Crowley, used to say that 'if they're not green and growing, they're ripe and rotting'. She was referring to the truism that if people are not learning, they're stagnating and falling into either apathy or stress, and neither of those places is good for them, for the people around them, or for the business.

THE PERFORMANCE EDGE

Living a life of full engagement is living at our performance edge.

> Our performance edge is where capacity meets challenge; where performance meets potential.

Like camping on the edge of a mountain, our performance edge is uncomfortable, yet exhilarating. It's challenging, yet gratifying. It's where we measure our character and put our strengths to work. It's where we discover who we are, what we are and why we are.

At our performance edge, we are dynamically changing via the interaction with a task and the environment. We are actively learning by doing; increasing our capacity, and expanding our potential. We are acquiring new knowledge and skills, which allows us to take on more responsibility or tasks of greater complexity.

The following diagram is my adapted version of the classic Flow Model, first presented by Mihaly Csikszentmihalyi (pronounced 'cheeks-a-men-i-hi') – with a few tweaks.

Csikszentmihalyi introduced the concept of flow as a mental state of operation in which a person is fully absorbed in an activity that requires both skill and challenge. In flow, we are lost in the moment. We forget about time. We forget everything except the task we are actively engaged in performing. People find flow in activities such as playing a musical instrument, designing a new concept, writing code, performing intricate surgery, cooking, painting, or any other activity that requires effort and focus.

Finding the performance edge

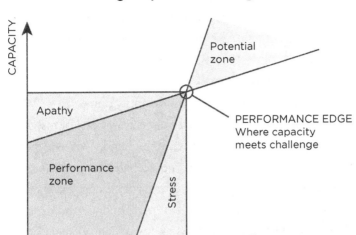

Let's have a look at the different elements of this diagram.

Capacity and challenge

In their *New York Times* bestseller *The Power of Full Engagement*, Jim Loehr and Tony Schwartz defined capacity as 'a function of one's ability to expand and recover energy'. Our capacity is our energy, and energy is our most important resource.

In their book they present four important principles to living a life of full engagement:

1. Full engagement requires drawing on four separate but related sources of energy: physical, emotional, mental and spiritual.

2. Because energy capacity diminishes both with overuse and with underuse, we must balance energy expenditure with energy renewal.

3. To build capacity, we must push beyond our normal limits, training in the same systematic way that elite athletes do.

4. Positive energy rituals – specific rituals for managing energy – are the key to full engagement and sustained high performance.

Based on these principles, capacity and challenge work as a team.

Capacity encompasses the full range of internal resources available to us, including mental, emotional, physical and spiritual resources (like our values and beliefs). We increase capacity by adapting to periodic cycles of stretch and renewal; integrating new skills and knowledge with each round; and harnessing our energy reserves.

Challenge is the difficulty level we apply ourselves to. We increase challenge by increasing complexity of task or scope of responsibility.

Challenge and capacity go hand in hand – as we increase our capacity, we are able to take on more challenging work. And as we take on more challenging work, our capacity increases. They feed each other, fostering a continuous cycle of performance and development.

When we are charged with work for which we have little skill or knowledge – when challenge outweighs capacity – we experience stress. Short bursts of stress are necessary for learning. But prolonged stress without adequate rest depletes energy reserves and damages performance.

For example, you wouldn't ask a junior lawyer to lead a high-profile case. You build that lawyer up over time with training and experiences. As the lawyer learns more, they take on not just more complex cases, but leadership responsibilities of the firm and empowerment to foster policy change within their chosen sector. They continually extend their capacity to meet ever-increasing challenges.

Conversely, when we are charged with work for which we are overqualified – when capacity outweighs challenge – we experience apathy. Apathy can also be sustained for short periods but is equally damaging to performance if prolonged. Like muscle atrophy, we deplete our capacity if we are not continually extending it.

For example, a father returning to work after parental leave may decide to take on a less challenging role to balance work and family demands. But a role that is underwhelming stalls learning and growth and becomes a demotivator, also damaging performance.

To increase capacity, we need to systematically increase the challenge, expending energy beyond normal levels. By upping the challenge and accepting new tasks or tasks of greater complexity, we move into the stress zone. But doing so systematically, following periods of stretch with periods of renewal, allows the learning to consolidate.

The performance zone

The performance zone is where we're comfortably challenged; performing a skill or doing work that we are familiar with, find stimulating, and for which we are actively using our strengths and talents. Just like the experience of flow described in the research of Mihaly Csikszentmihalyi, when we are in our performance zone we are fully engaged; delivering work to a high standard and adding significant value to customers, colleagues and our communities. Our work is challenging, but we know we're doing a great job and this fills us with an enormous sense of purpose and pride.

In the performance zone, we've reached a level of **unconscious competence**. Noel Burch introduced this concept in the late 1960s as the fourth rung on a ladder we climb when learning something new. Unconscious competence is a state of being where new skills are seamlessly integrated with our knowledge base and we perform them on autopilot. Like touch-typing – once you've learned how to do it, you no longer think about the keys but the words you are translating onto the screen.

Unconscious competence is preceded by:

- **unconscious incompetence** at the bottom of the learning ladder (when you don't know what you don't know)

- **conscious incompetence** at the next rung (when you know what you don't know)

- **conscious competence** on the third rung (knowing what you know)

- and then **unconscious competence** on the top rung (intuitive knowing).

The danger zone on the learning ladder is pushing past the discomfort of 'not knowing' in order to 'come to know'; of being okay with appearing to be incompetent for a short while at least while adapting to new ways of thinking and behaving. The fear of feeling and look-ing incompetent keeps many people from trying something new and stepping outside their comfort zones. But it's worth it – because the reward for this temporary form of vulnerability is a greater sense of competence and mastery in your chosen field.

The potential zone

When performance coaches claim to help you 'realise your potential', what do they actually mean? What is potential? Where does it sit in your body? Is it just a fluffy word?

> **Our potential zone is the place where learning and growth happen.**

Our potential zone is latent talent that has not yet been realised. I like to think about potential as connections in your brain that haven't happened yet. Realising potential means putting your skills and capa-bilities to work in new ways and strengthening brain interconnectivity.

More connections mean more processing power, granting us the capacity to think beyond the *concrete* to the *concept* and *context*. When we reach into our potential zone, we dig deep, forge new neural path-ways and make new connections. The brain is continuously evolving, and dendrites (the extensions of brain cells or neurons that look like tiny trees) never stop reaching for more connections. Pathways in the brain are constantly expanding, pruning and combining as new mem-ories and experiences are storing every living moment. Neuroscientists call this phenomenon 'brain plasticity'.

Throughout my studies in psychology and psychophysiology, I'd read about the whole spectrum of brain injury cases. There were cases where people recovered no function, partial function, and even full function following brain injury or surgery. But there were the occa-sional extraordinary cases where some people adapted to perform beyond pre-injury levels, which prove how continued effort and focus allow us to rebuild pathways in the brain.

I witnessed this firsthand when I met my husband's cousin, Trevor.

When Trevor was only 12 years old, he started suffering debilitating headaches, and the usually fun-loving boy with a passion for table tennis started acting out. His concerned parents took him for a series of tests, and were given the worst possible news – Trevor had a tumour near the centre of his brain and was given three months to live. Surgery was an option, but a risky one. His survival prospects were 50% at best, and he had only a 5% to 10% chance of emerging with all faculties and bodily functions intact. Clearly this was devastating news for the family, but Trevor didn't want to see his days deteriorating in a hospital bed, so he decided to give surgery a chance.

Trevor did survive the surgery – and in fact did much more than that. He was home 10 days later, and despite continuing headaches and temporary loss of sight in his right eye, he picked up the table tennis bat and started playing again. Within three months, his recovery reached the stage his parents expected would take 12 months. Trevor went on to become a table tennis champion, representing Australia in the Commonwealth Games in 2002 and 2006 and the Athens Olympics in 2004. Trevor married a French girl Lise while playing professionally in France, returned to Australia, completed a PhD in neuroscience, and now works in the field that saved his life. Trevor and Lise have three healthy, beautiful children, all budding athletes.

Trevor's remarkable story is one of incredible resilience to rebuild the pathways in his brain as well as pathways in his life through the dynamic game of table tennis.

At a metaphysical level, we reach into our potential zone when we push past the edge of what we know, to the *unthought known*. They are the things we *know* but haven't yet *thought*. The unthought known was a concept introduced by psychoanalyst Christopher Bollas to represent experiences which are felt in us and formed prior to the development of language at around the age of three. These felt experiences live within your pre-conscious mind, your emotional memory, until they are surfaced by later experiences and ultimately 'thought'. When we experience unthought knowns, we are reaching our potential because we are making sense of early emotional memories based on new experiences, and this raises our level of conscious competence.

The apathy zone

The apathy zone is where capacity outweighs challenge. We have adapted to the change, mastered the role, the project, the new KPI; and it is no longer challenging. We experience this state when we have been in the same role for too long, take on a lesser role, or get pigeonholed (tasked with the same things over and over because we're good at it). This zone causes energy depletion, but not because we are overdrawing on energy reserves, because we are *under*drawing on them. Like muscles not being used, our capacity starts to atrophy. If you don't use it – you lose it!

The stress zone

The stress zone is where challenge outweighs capacity. We are pushed past our current capacity and must overdraw on internal energy reserves. We experience this state when we experience unanticipated changes, adopt new challenges, new roles, promotions, or increase the stakes on existing roles. This level of performance draws down heavily on internal resources – our physical, mental and emotional energy reserves. Working in this zone for extended stretches puts us in a depleted state, creates risk and damages safety. We can only sustain performance if we incorporate periods of rest and learn essential skills and knowledge that allow us to meet a challenge and move back into our performance zone. This is why we invest in people to grow our businesses. When people grow, business grows. It's a win–win for everyone.

***

Living at our performance edge is a dynamic process of learning that takes place at the individual, team and organisational level.

> The challenge for leaders and changemakers is helping
> individuals and teams to discover their performance edge
> and safely hold them there.

If we up the challenge without investing in people's capacity to cope, we push them into the stress zone. But if we don't up the challenge and let people stagnate, we risk losing them from apathy and boredom.

2

Understanding systems

ORGANISATIONS ARE OPEN SYSTEMS

So, let's go back to basics for a moment. What exactly *is* a system? A system has two definitions:

1. A set of things working together as parts of a mechanism or an interconnecting network; a complex whole.

2. A set of principles or procedures according to which something is done; an organised scheme or method.

If you are dealing with an organisational system – a complex network of interconnecting parts – you need a set of principles and processes to improve how those parts work together. This book provides you with the system for organisational performance, so that *your* system has an improved capacity to convert imports into higher value exports.

Depending on your organisation, *your* system could be:

- a system for fitness (for example, personal trainers)

- a system for unity of mind, body and spirit (for example, yoga schools)

- a system for personal digital and communications technology (for example, Apple)

- a system for measuring workplace engagement (for example, Culture Amp).

Regardless of whether you're selling a product (cereal, vitamins, shoes, music, cars, furniture), a service (consulting, therapy, healthcare, IT support, cleaning) or a system, to be a high-performing team you need to focus on your *systems of performance*.

GROUP DYNAMICS

Let me paint you a picture. I'm sitting in a room with chairs set up in an open circle, with 25 other people. No, it's not group therapy (although at the time it felt like it!). It's a group of mature-age students joining together for their first class of a three-year masters program in Organisation Dynamics. While we've already had basic introductions to one another and established a tentative level of familiarity, this class is our first formal learning encounter together.

The professor – who joins us in the circle – declares that our task for the next 60 minutes is to study the group dynamic as it occurs. This session will be voice recorded. There will be 10 of these sessions – one for each week of the semester. Our assignment will be to choose just 15 minutes of one session and write a 3000-word thesis on what was playing out in the group dynamic in that 15-minute segment.

That's it. Study the group dynamic. As. It. Occurs. For one hour. Time starts. Then … silence.

Hearts pumping. Seats shifting. Legs crossing and uncrossing. Palms getting sweaty. Eyes rapidly scanning then landing back on the carpet in the centre of the circle – which has suddenly become very interesting to everyone.

I've never before realised that silence could be so unbearably *loud!* My mind is non-stop chattering to mask feelings of deep vulnerability … *Who will speak first? What is there to say? Should I ease the tension with a joke? What will that say about me? What if the joke is offensive to someone? I don't want to speak first. But someone has to speak – or we'll have nothing to talk about for an hour. What does that say about the group dynamic? ...* on and on the internal dialogue went.

What this activity was highlighting was the actual existence of a group dynamic. The group dynamic is not something we usually see; like a shadow, it only appears when we cast light upon it.

> **Group life is deep, rich, layered and textured.**

Seeing a group as a whole, instead of the sum of its parts, helps us understand that groups have their own life. They are more than the sum of their parts, because of what's created when the parts interact.

Groups form primarily to perform a function. Researcher Albert Kenneth Rice called this their 'primary task' – or the function they must perform to survive. Play basketball. Create a Strategic Plan. Design a new product. Clean a building. Teach a class. Perform surgery. Celebrate a birthday. Usually, we let the task take centre stage, while the group dynamic quietly goes about its business, working its magic behind the scenes – raising and lowering the curtain on the main act.

But in that class, our task was to *study* the group dynamic. We had nowhere else to go. There it was, plain as day, terrifying in its nakedness!

The work system and the human system

Eric Trist and Ken Bamforth first wrote about the concept of two systems at play in groups in the 1950s following their studies of men working in coal mines. They coined the term 'socio-technical systems'. The technical system includes the machinery, the technology, and the proprietary process or intellectual property that results in the product or service. The social system is the people and their interpersonal relationships that allow for collaboration and task completion. I think of these as the 'work system' and the 'human system'. The elements of each system are shown in the following table.

The 'work system' and the 'human system' at play in group life

Work system	Human system
Tasks	People
Outputs	Relationships
Physical tools and equipment	Mental skills and competencies
Systems and processes	Roles and role boundaries
Actions and behaviours	Thoughts and feelings
Visible	Invisible

The group dynamic is the interplay of these two systems. One affects the other, and the effectiveness of the whole depends on the balance between them.

> When we talk about workflow, we're actually referring to the work flowing through the human system. If the human system is blocked, the work is stopped.

It may be, and often is, that a system has to work below its optimum capacity in order to maintain a balance of what is sustainable in the human system. For example, when I worked as a management consultant, our average 'target utilisation rate' on projects was 75%. That is, the benchmark for performance was to spend 75% of time on client projects. The other 25% was committed to seeking new opportunities, building client relationships, professional development and project administration – all necessary activities that generated more work, strengthened connectedness of the social group, enabled learning, and fostered a positive workplace experience. Working consistently at 100% 'billable hours' was neither promoted nor desired, because the compounding effect of the cost to the human system would eventually undermine performance in the work system and ultimately lead to system collapse.

'Maximising productivity' does not mean working people harder. It actually means finding the right balance between the work system and the human system that sustains long-term high performance.

OPEN VERSUS CLOSED SYSTEMS

Year 12 biology class was the first time I was introduced to the wondrous and marvellous design of a single human cell. Cells are the basic building blocks of all living things. Our understanding of how human cells and biological processes work was enabled by the theories of an Austrian biologist from the 1960s: Ludwig von Bertalanffy (I always loved his name – sounds like 'butterfly'). He is recognised for his development of general systems theory, and in particular the concept of an 'open' system. It was not until his contributions in his seminal essay in 1969 that systems were studied as a discrete concept.

Von Bertalanffy introduced the concept of an open system and a closed system:

- A **closed system** is one that operates independently of its environment. A battery, a car engine, and a kettle are all examples of closed systems.

- An **open system** is continually in contact with its environment, importing energy, converting, and then exporting the transformed energy back into the environment. All living organisms like plants, animals and human beings are open systems, as are non-living systems that exchange both heat and matter with the environment (such as a boiling pot with no lid).

A human cell is a perfect open system. Its basic function is to take nutrients from food, convert those nutrients into energy, and export transformed energy back into the body. It achieves a steady state by maintaining a balance between itself and the environment. Cells contain our DNA and can make copies of themselves. They are perfect little parcels from which all evolution has spawned.

Like human cells, organisations are open systems that import energy, people and materials; complete an internal value-add process; and export products and services back into the environment.

Organisations are open systems

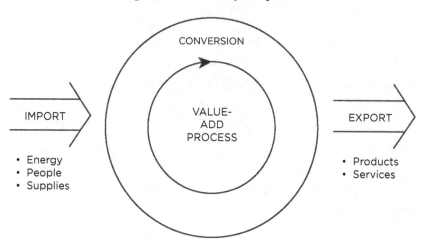

Albert Kenneth Rice was the first researcher in the 1960s to apply the metaphor of an open system to organisations following his work with an Indian textile mill – now famously known in Group Relations circles as the 'Ahmedabad Experiment'. His work built upon the foundations of socio-technical systems theory proposed earlier by Trist and Bamforth.

BOUNDARY MANAGEMENT IN OPEN SYSTEMS

All systems have boundaries, and in an open system 'boundary management' becomes an important consideration.

In cells, a permeable membrane manages the import and export of essential components necessary for maintaining a steady state. In organisations, managers play a similar role at the boundary, making decisions about: what comes in (people, supplies, new concepts);

how the work moves through the various subsystems; is converted; and is then delivered as a value-added product or service.

Managers balance not only the interplay between subsystems, they also balance the interplay between inside and outside the organisation, with their most important role being to ensure adaptiveness and responsiveness to changes in the external environment.

Leaders effectively maintain boundaries by providing clarity on goals and expectations for performance. They define the level of output required to meet the organisation's mission and strategy. They source the inputs necessary to convert to outputs. They determine the pace and procedure of the conversion process. Leaders play an important role in deciding both what they can commit to and what to say no to – keeping teams focused on high value-adding actions and processes that deliver a strong return on investment (ROI).

ADAPT OR DIE

Because organisations maintain effectiveness via a continual process of interaction with their environment, their survival depends on how well they adapt.

Unlike a human cell, organisations rarely exist to simply maintain a steady state. The goal for many is to grow, to influence change, to make the lives of their customers and communities better in the service of their purpose. Sometimes, organisations disrupt the very environments in which they operate. They are game changers.

When this happens, their competitors face a decision: adapt or die. Sometimes they don't realise this until it's too late. The table overleaf lists some examples of companies that changed the game, and some that failed to keep up.

> **Your organisation does not exist in a vacuum. It exists in a dynamically changing market, influenced by fluctuations in the broader social, political and environmental context.**

**Companies that changed the game and
some that failed to keep up**

Five companies that changed markets	Five companies that failed to adapt
Fuji – with digital cameras	**Kodak** – failed to adapt from photographic film and printing
Netflix – with on-demand streaming	**Blockbuster** – failed to adapt from video and game rental
Amazon – with online retailing	**Sears** – failed to adapt early enough from bricks-and-mortar retailing
Facebook – with user-led social media platform design	**MySpace** – failed to adapt key features like seeing real friends versus anonymous friends
Apple – with touch-screen technology	**Blackberry** – failed to adapt from touch-type keyboards

Without a clear understanding of the symbiotic nature of the relationship between your organisation and your environment, the organisation will struggle to survive, let alone lead market change.

3

How good systems amplify performance

WHEN THINGS DON'T WORK OUT

The struggle to work out why new initiatives, changes or training programs are not working is something every manager experiences. Let's consider some examples.

A new hire who doesn't fit

Amy is the General Manager of a mid-sized organic beverage company. The company has grown to a size that warrants hiring a new Head of Sales to lead the sales team and gain entry into new international markets. Amy hires Rick – who has come from a larger corporate fast-moving consumer goods (FMCG) company and is now taking a smaller role to find a better work–life integration. Amy notices that Rick seems at odds with the culture. He spends lots of time at his desk, uses corporate language, and relies heavily on email. When Rick puts forward a new strategy, he struggles to gain buy-in from his peers in the leadership team. Without support from Marketing and Operations, Rick's strategies won't be successful, and it is not Amy's style to enforce decisions. Amy decides Rick is not delivering the value she expected from someone at his salary level, so she regrettably lets him go before his probation is over.

Training that doesn't seem to work

Nick is the Head of People and Culture at a hospitality company. Nick is run off his feet getting around to all the venues to deal with the people challenges that keep popping up. He seems to be on a constant churn of hiring and firing and can't keep good staff in the venues. This is affecting the customer experience. Nick decides to invest in leadership training for his venue managers so they can properly recruit, induct, train and give feedback, and stem the flow of turnover. Nick pays for a customised blended training program – knowing that it needs to be relevant and accessible to gain maximum participation. Six months after the program, Nick does not notice any change to turnover or in the number of incidents he is attending to. He is disappointed the training did not deliver the value it promised.

A new system not being taken up

John runs a construction company. He has invested time and effort working with his senior team to create a five-year Strategic Plan that can be communicated to the whole business and used by all his managers to set goals and KPIs across the team. To support this process, he implemented an online performance management system to capture individual goals and learning plans, and he trained every manager in how to use the system. Once this was in place, John turned his mind to focusing on securing new construction projects to fill the pipeline. Three months has now gone by, and John is frustrated to see that only about 50% of the organisation has recorded performance goals in the system and only 25% are having monthly performance conversations. When he raises his frustration with his leadership team, their excuse is that their people think these conversations are distracting them from core projects and having a negative effect on productivity.

Unmet expectations

Ann runs a non-for-profit community centre. She has a team of contractors who deliver weekly education sessions for young women in the community. As well-intentioned as they are, there are a couple of contractors who aren't meeting performance expectations. Ann knows she needs to make their roles clearer, so she sets up monthly catch-ups where she communicates the projects and deliverables she's expecting from each of them, and can give them honest and timely feedback. After three months of these meetings, Ann is realising that the contractors still behave as if her expectations are optional. To save herself money and time, she decides to take on some of the work herself, so lets one of the contractors go. Six months later, Ann has not had the time to put in funding applications that would have given them the opportunity to expand their operation to an online format.

* * *

Do any of these sound familiar? How many times have you experienced …

- A new hire who doesn't fit?

- A training program that does not improve behaviour?

- A new system that is not taken up?

- A set of expectations that aren't met?

- A change program that does not stick?

- A strategy that is not implemented?

- A set of company values that aren't demonstrated?

- A new process that people don't follow?

The problem in the above cases wasn't that people weren't talented enough, or the training program wasn't powerful enough, or the technology wasn't good enough, or the feedback wasn't clear enough. The problem is that if you are effecting change in one part of the system, you need to think about how those parts connect and if the other parts of the system also serve the change you are working to create.

The problem is that there was no **system of performance** to plug these new initiatives into. Your performance system is like the vascular system of your organisation – like blood, it carries vital information, resources, tools and skills into the interrelated subsystems so they can be absorbed by teams and individuals, used to add value and converted into better performance. When systems of performance are integrated in an organisation, a new change or initiative has a network to flow through.

> **Once you have performance systems in place, adapting, changing and responding to opportunities or shifts in the market becomes easy.**

Instead of you doing the work, the system does the work for you.

UNDERSTANDING INTEGRATED SYSTEMS

My son, Byron, is fond of Lego. Who isn't? It's a fantastic toy and we have boxes of the stuff. For his ninth birthday he received from Grandpa a set for a bright orange Corvette with black stripes down the side. The recommended age for this was 12 to 14 years. Byron was ecstatic to be trusted with such a momentous challenge. He set to work. He spent days working on it, building it in stages. Finally he put the last pieces in and set his car in motion. When it rolled, the pistons were supposed to go up and down. But alas, no pistons were pumping. He descended into tears of frustration. He set it aside for a few days, before coming back at it with renewed vigour. He pulled it apart almost to the beginning, and started building it again. This time around, the pistons pumped.

When parts don't connect, they don't work. Or, like Byron's first build, they only partially achieve their potential. Organisational systems are much the same. Organisations are composed of interrelated subsystems. They are like Russian Dolls, containing wholes within wholes. Organisations have individuals (who are systems of their own account), who belong to teams, who belong to departments, who belong to work areas, and so on. For the whole organisation to perform as it should, the subsystems need to find points of alignment.

If they only partially connect, they deliver mediocre performance. If they fully connect and fully align, they deliver high performance. Integrated systems create the optimal internal conditions that amplify performance.

The nature of your organisational system directly impacts where people focus their energy and effort, which ultimately impacts market performance. The more interconnected the systems of leadership, culture and strategy are, the stronger your market performance will be.

Where the focus goes, the energy flows and the value grows

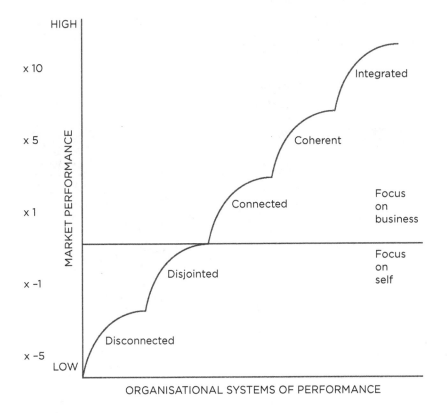

ORGANISATIONAL SYSTEMS OF PERFORMANCE

The nature of the organisational system influences how we think, feel and act.

This idea lies at the very heart of organisation dynamics.

In **disconnected** and **disjointed** systems, people will waste effort and energy on self-protection instead of getting on with the task. The human system becomes the focal point of energy. Organisations with disconnected or disjointed systems deliver sub-average market performance.

In **connected**, **coherent**, and **integrated** systems, people are enabled to bring their full selves to the completion of their work. The business becomes the focal point of energy. Connected systems meet market performance, while coherent and integrated systems deliver superior market performance.

The following table summarises how the nature of the organisational system influences the direction of our energy and effort.

**How the nature of the system influences
the direction of energy and effort**

	Organisational system	Focus on	Effort	Market performance
Focus on business	Integrated	Continuous improvement	Amplified	× 10
	Coherent	Task performance	Sustained	× 5
	Connected	Task completion	Applied	× 1
Focus on self	Disjointed	Internal competition	Scattered	× -1
	Disconnected	Self-protection	Withheld	× -5

Let's have a look at each of these, starting from the bottom up.

Disconnected systems

My family and I are very lucky to live in a home that backs onto a nature reserve. Every day we wake up looking into a wall of trees. When we first moved here, however, there were two pine trees right on the fence line. One was at a sharp angle – leaning into the other, which was propping it up. They were a real danger to all of us, including my boys and my neighbours' boys who played in the yard often.

My neighbour called the council several times. He kept getting the runaround – being transferred to the wrong department, leaving messages that were never returned. We were both feeling frustrated and angry about the situation. I decided to change tack and appeal to someone's kindness to help us out. I rang the council number and started my campaign with the receptionist. I shared with her my fear for our safety, the fact that we'd had no luck getting onto anyone in the council, and that I was genuinely in her hands and could she please help me. She put me on hold while she rang around the departments to find out who could speak to me right there and then. She transferred me to another lovely woman. I shared the same story, and this woman listened. I don't know what department she was in, but she assured me she would get onto it.

To my great relief, I received a call back the next day to inform me that tree guys were coming out to assess the situation. To my even greater relief, they turned up *that day*! They took one look at the trees, scratched their heads, and agreed, 'Yep … they've gotta go'. The next week, an arborist arrived, and finally those two portents of disaster were taken away. Now we can all enjoy our backyard in safety and peace.

In **disconnected** systems, the parts simply don't connect. People are focused on **self-protection**. They adopt an 'if it's not in my job description, then it's not my problem' mentality. Until someone *makes* it their problem. Like I did, gently, with those women on the other end of the phone that day. In these systems, effort is **withheld**, resulting in underperformance because individuals and teams fail to meet the expectations of customers and the business will quickly lose market share, or in the case of a council – lose votes.

Disconnected organisational systems are like Lego boxes with critical parts missing. They simply can't come together, and they cause the builder no end of frustration, disappointment and stress.

Disjointed systems

In a software development company I worked with, the sales, operations and development teams struggled to align, and even at times expressed open hostility towards each other. Two years prior, the developers had presented a new software upgrade they were working on that was going to revolutionise their customers' productivity. They predicted the timeline in which the package was going to be ready. The sales team prepared sales presentations, revised sales strategies, and went out to market. The product was met positively and customers were keen.

At the predicted timeline, the product wasn't ready. The sales team placated customers. Still, more months went by – and more development needed to be done. In the meantime, the legacy system was causing challenges and putting extra pressure on the operations team to patch things up while continuing a full workload of installations on other products. The sales and operations teams were fielding customer complaints.

Internal tension was becoming destructive to the company culture. The CEO couldn't understand why these three critical areas of the business couldn't align. They blamed each other for the problem that had been caused. The developers blamed sales for taking the product to market before it was ready. The sales team blamed the developers for failing to complete the project to their own projected timelines. The operations team blamed both for thinking it was all going to be easy. To the executive team and many of the employees, the place felt like a warzone.

That was an experience of working with a **disjointed** system. In disjoined systems, some parts are connected, while others are not. In disjointed systems, we put more pressure on the human system because we resort to relying on the social and influencing skills of people to work *around* the system, not *through* the system, to get things done. In these systems, people are focused on **internal competition**; getting their own part done and making sure they meet the expectations of management, while blaming others and keeping their heads down when the parts don't line up or things go wrong.

In these systems, effort is **scattered**; sometimes effort equals results, sometimes effort equals no results. The impact of effort in these systems is unpredictable, and ultimately this leads to under-performance compared to market benchmarks.

Connected systems

In **connected** systems, all parts in the system are interconnected with each other. Individuals have clarity on goals, roles and responsibilities, and how all the parts work together as a whole. In connected systems, the focus is on **task completion**, and effort is **applied**. People are enabled to bring their energy to their work and focus on completing tasks with a level of confidence that their efforts will align with the efforts of their teammates and will translate to results.

Connected systems are very successful at engaging in what business theorist Chris Argyris described in the 1970s as 'single-loop learning'. Single-loop learning is the ability to scan the environment, set objectives, and monitor performance in relation to set objectives. In single-loop learning, individuals and groups adjust their behaviour relative to fixed goals, norms, and assumptions.

Connected systems perform well in markets and environments that are relatively stable, or where there is little external competition. Public hospitals, public schools, libraries, and the military are examples of systems that perform well if they remain focused on internal improvement and achievement of self-set goals.

Coherent systems

Coherent systems go one step further than connected systems by focusing on adapting their internal mechanisms based on shifting external trends in the populations or markets they serve.

Stone & Wood Brewing Company is an independent brewing company based in the Northern Rivers of New South Wales. Founded by three former colleagues at Carlton & United Breweries in 2008, Jamie Cook, Brad Rogers and Ross Jurisich were inspired by the idea of creating a village brewery with the vision of building a conscious business. To keep themselves focused on this vision, they created what they called the Stone & Wood Family Wheel. The Family Wheel is a circle with seven segments pictured like seven slices of pie, each one representing a key stakeholder group: community, environment, team, suppliers, drinkers, customers and shareholders.

Stone & Wood use the wheel to guide strategy creation – ensuring they have strategies in place that enable them to add value to every stakeholder group. This process not only keeps them accountable to their vision, but connected to and relevant in their market.

Stone & Wood are a great example of a coherent system, where not only are all internal parts connected to each other, but the organisation as a whole is deeply connected within its market and operating context. In these organisations, people focus on **task performance**, and their effort is **sustained**. They break free of bureaucratic thinking and organise in ways that meet the shifting requirements of the environment in order to not just meet but exceed market performance.

The focus in coherent systems is not just achievement, but adaptation. They are very good at what Argyris called 'double-loop learning'. Double-loop learning involves a double task – that of both monitoring the organisation's progress relative to its goals, norms and assumptions, as well as the process of questioning the relevance of these goals, norms and assumptions in light of ongoing changes in the operating environment.

These organisations outperform market competitors, because they are agile, responsive, and relevant in their markets. In their tenth year, independent brewer Stone & Wood grew from their regional home base to exceed an annual production of 12 million litres, an achievement few other independent Australian breweries have come close to.

Integrated systems

In **integrated** organisations, people focus on **continuous improvement** and their effort is **amplified**. Integrated organisations amplify performance because they have systems in place which enable them to be market disruptors. They engage in *triple-loop* learning, where there is a tri-focus on continuous improvement:

1. Achieve self-set goals.

2. Adapt to shifting market conditions.

3. Disrupt to create new solutions to existing customer problems.

The tri-focus of integrated systems

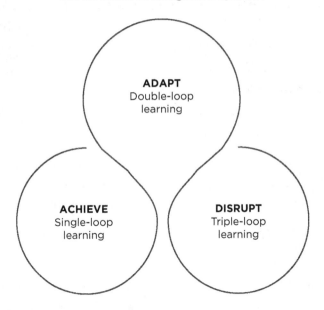

3M are widely recognised as an industry-leading company. Founded in 1902, the company is a global conglomerate producing thousands of products, and is a world leader in markets from health care and highway safety to office products, abrasives, and adhesives. In 2020, they were ranked 103 on the Fortune 500 list, employing over 95,000 employees with global sales of US$32 billion.

3M attributes its success to five key areas:

1. **Feeling their customers' pain:** 3M look for and listen to customer pain points. Customers' problems are 3M's solutions.

2. **Empowering employees:** 3M allow employees to work on what they are passionate about. They promote innovative ideas and reward people for them.

3. **Dedicating time to innovation:** In 1948, 3M launched its now famous 15% program – where 15% of employee time is dedicated to innovation. When innovative ideas make it through the ideation phase, employees are given technology grants to pursue these ideas. The Post-It Note was invented during 15% time. Organisations such as Hewlett-Packard and Google have replicated this approach. Gmail and Google Earth were conceived during Google's 15% time. While people are encouraged to work on their ideas, they must complete their billable work first, making the opportunity to innovate a core motivator for people in the organisation.

4. **Collaborative platforms:** 3M use social media technologies to promote collaboration and ideas sharing across the organisation, harnessing the collective intelligence of their people.

5. **Talented people:** 3M showcase their innovations as an attraction and retention strategy for top talent.

3M has mastered the art of organisational integration. In addition to being deeply interconnected with all stakeholder groups both internally and externally, integrated organisations are industry disruptors. Like 3M with the Post-It, Netflix with on-demand streaming, and Apple with touch-screen technology, these companies are focused on continuous improvement and exist to make the lives of customers better by anticipating what their customers want before they even know that they want it.

MAKE YOUR SYSTEM WORK FOR YOU

James Clear, author of *Atomic Habits*, says that if you want to improve your life and enhance your personal performance, set a goal, but focus on your habits: 'Goals are about the results you want to achieve. Systems are about the processes that lead to those results.'

James talks about the power of an 'atomic habit' – a regular practice or routine that is small and easy to do, and compounds over time. For example, if you aim to get just 1% better each day, you'll end up with results that are 37 times better after one year. What starts with a small change adds up to a big gain.

In the same way, focusing on the system, rather than the goal of change, is the fundamental process that contributes to overall improvement.

> **If habits are the smallest units of behaviour that contribute to overall performance, then systems are the scaffolding that support high-performance cultures.**

As James says, 'You do not rise to the level of your goals. You fall to the level of your systems.' Systems provide leaders with the framework required to uphold performance across an entire organisation. Once you have a system in place, you can let it do the work for you.

Improving the conversion rate of your value-add process

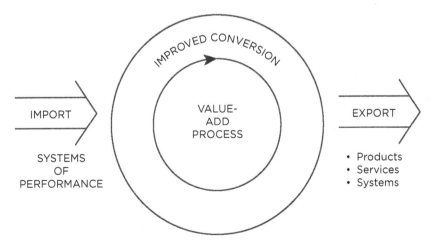

By creating high-performance systems, you improve the conversion rate of your internal value-add process, exporting products and services at better quality, lower cost or higher speed.

4

Introducing
The High-Performance System

Austrian-born American management consultant Peter Drucker is the father of modern corporate philosophy. Drucker is famous for saying that 'culture eats strategy for breakfast'.

I'm going out on a limb here and saying that Drucker was wrong. Here's why:

1. Culture and strategy are equally important.

2. He missed a third, also equally important factor: leadership.

3. *Omne trium perfectum* – Latin for 'everything that is three is perfect'.

> **Culture, strategy and leadership are the holy trinity of high performance.**

And they are in good company. All good things come in threes. Three blind mice; three little pigs; three bears. In Kabbalah philosophy the number three signifies harmony. To the Chinese, three is a lucky number. The rule of three has applications in aesthetics. Three is the lowest number of entities to form a pattern.[1]

---

1 Check out Steve Dayan, MD who published a comprehensive article on the phenomenon of threes on www.modernaesthetics.com titled 'Omne Trium Perfectum'.

THE HIGH-PERFORMANCE SYSTEM

Leadership, culture and strategy are the three critical elements that connect the activities of people across the whole of your organisation. They are the organising principles that determine what people work on and how they work together to achieve the potential of your business.

This book is *not* about how you set up an operating system, or a marketing system, or an innovation system. This book is about how you can *successfully align these* into the following cross-functional systems:

- **The Leadership System**, which becomes your process for inspiring high performance and developing the capacity of your people to continuously improve.

- **The Culture System**, which becomes your process for ensuring there is a high degree of alignment between your espoused values and your lived values in the service of shared purpose.

- **The Strategy System**, which becomes your process for strategy creation and strategy execution that ensures your organisation remains adaptive and relevant in your chosen market.

These systems should be designed into your organisation to create the conditions for people and teams to work at peak performance (or their performance edge). The High-Performance System is the successful combination of these.

The outcome of these systems is the 3Ps of high-performing organisations: **Purpose**, **Passion** and **Performance**.

Together, the net result of an organisation where people are connected to purpose, passionate about what they do, and performing to a high standard is *profit*.

Purpose + Passion + Performance = Profit

Think of it like a fidget spinner – one of the hottest toys of 2019. If you don't know what they are – they're small ball-bearing devices with three 'wings'. You hold them at the centre, and with the slightest application of force, set them into a spinning motion that lasts for ages. The ball bearings are the key to the spinning motion; they reduce friction and allow the wings to rotate freely for a long time. Friction, in simple terms, is the resistance to motion that occurs when one object moves against another. Less friction equals sustained momentum.

The systems work together to reduce friction, and when spinning smoothly create their own momentum that fuels purpose, passion and performance.

The elements of The High-Performance System are shown in the following image.

The High-Performance System

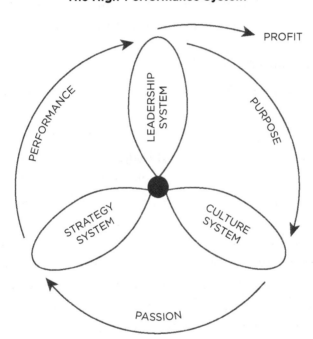

Let's have a closer look.

LEADERSHIP fuels PURPOSE

Leaders do the work of inspiring high performance by keeping people connected to the purpose of the organisation.

The purpose is the organisation's reason for being – it is the problem you solve or the need you fulfil in the market. Unless your organisation serves a meaningful purpose, it ceases to be relevant. The real power of purpose comes through maintaining the collective connection to it. Simon Sinek, international speaker and author of the highly influential book *Start with Why*, says it best, telling us that 'people don't buy *what* you do, they buy *why* you do it'. This is true for internal customers as well as external customers.

Unless leaders continually create context to connect people to their purpose within the team, the team to their purpose within the business, and the business to its purpose within the market, the power of purpose to motivate and inspire people becomes lost.

CULTURE fuels PASSION

Culture fuels passion by connecting people to a shared system of values and beliefs.

Human Synergistics, a global organisation providing research and measurement tools for culture and leadership, defines culture as 'the shared values, norms and expectations that govern the way people approach their work and interact with each other'. Their research shows that when there exists a high degree of alignment between your 'ideal culture' (your espoused values and beliefs) and your 'actual culture' (the experience employees have every day) there are strong outcomes at the individual, team and organisation levels. That is, people are more engaged, demonstrate better teamwork, and deliver better quality outcomes than organisations that do not live their espoused values.

In business cultures with lots of passion, people really care about what they do. They get excited about just being at work and they share this excitement with each other. And passion is felt by the customer. When your people talk about your products and services with passion to your customers, they can't help but feel excited too. Passion is a positive, inspiring force, that motivates people to sustain momentum even when things get difficult. Passion is contagious.

STRATEGY fuels PERFORMANCE

Strategy fuels performance by ensuring all team members set and are accountable to results.

It's true that leaders have a very special linking and leading role in this framework. Leaders create and execute strategy through their teams. Leaders also reinforce the culture through their actions and behaviours. However, culture and strategy belong to more than just the leaders of the organisation, or those with delegated authority. Culture is lived and demonstrated through every person in an organisation. Likewise, every person plays an important part in the creation and execution of strategy.

So leaders are certainly an important lynchpin in the whole framework, but they are by no means the only ones who are involved in the process of becoming a high-performing team. In high-performing teams and high-performing organisations, followership is just as important as leadership. Great followers make great leaders, and vice versa.

PROFIT is the OUTCOME

Profit is not the *reason* we do business. Profit is the *outcome* of doing business well. Some people think that profit is a dirty word. It's not. I've worked in organisations that have profit as one of their core values; they are industry leaders and employers of choice.

Profit is a critical measure of a healthy system. A system that can sustain itself, operate independently and increase its influence. Even in non-for-profits, any 'profit' generated by donations or grants is effectively an opportunity to expand the reach of the service or provide extra support to the community.

Profit is the life-giving blood of an organisation – it keeps the system flowing and growing. Profit is the result of a clearly defined purpose, fuelling passion among all stakeholder groups, driving performance and measurable results.

***

> **Without building systems for these three critical organising and aligning processes, organisational leaders leave performance up to chance.**

They put themselves, their teams and their business at risk by relying on memory or sheer force of will, and this is not a reliable or sustainable approach. Systems create habits which create results. The High-Performance System is a proven process for amplifying performance by successfully integrating your systems for leadership, culture and strategy.

Part I summary

- To thrive in a VUCA world, we need to build organisations that are adaptive and resilient.

- High-performing teams effectively leverage collective capacity to achieve team synergy – where the whole is greater than the sum of the parts.

- Our performance edge is where capacity meets challenge, where performance meets potential. Living a life of full engagement is living at our performance edge.

- Organisations are open systems that maintain effectiveness via a continual process of exchange with their environment. Optimal performance depends on how well they adapt to changing market conditions.

- Integrated systems amplify performance by maximising the value-add input, conversion, and output process.

- High performance is a system. Systems create habits which create results. Let the system do the work for you.

- High-performance systems are processes designed into organisations that create the perfect conditions for teams to work at their performance edge.

- The Leadership System is the process for inspiring high performance and developing the capacities of people to continuously learn, grow and improve.

- The Culture System is the process for living your values at every stage of the employee lifecycle and for prioritising the wellbeing of your people.

- The Strategy System is your process for aligning on goals and targets to remain relevant within your market, and continually monitoring your progress towards goals and standards.

- High-performance systems create their own momentum that drive the 3Ps: leadership fuels purpose, strategy fuels performance, culture fuels passion.

- Together, purpose, passion and performance = profit.

- Profit is the result of doing business well. Profit is the life-giving blood of the business – it keeps the system flowing and growing.

Part II

The Leadership System

'Those who truly lead are able to create a following
of people who act not because they were swayed,
but because they were inspired.'

Simon Sinek, *Start with Why*

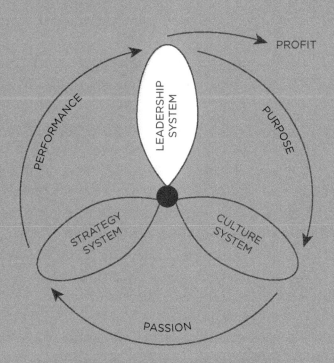

FIVE-2-FIFTY AT HAWTHORN FOOTBALL CLUB

Sport can provide us with great examples to draw on in the business world. The journey, failures and successes sporting clubs experience are so public for all to see that in some ways they feel familiar and known to us. Even if we're not sports fans ourselves, we have all witnessed a great, inspiring act of leadership on the sporting field that we can learn from in business.

I have a very personal insight into how Australian Rules Football (AFL) team Hawthorn Football Club rose from the ashes in the mid 2000s following a decade of poor performance. My husband, Clinton Bown, was part of the senior executive team that saw the club from languishing around the bottom of the ladder to become one of the most dominant clubs in the modern era of AFL.

Following years of success in the 1970s, 1980s and early 1990s, Hawthorn's performance spiralled downward. It was bereft of any of the grit that had seen it so admired, and lacked the clear leadership required to see it flourish. It got so bad that in 1996 the club almost merged with the Melbourne Football Club.

In 2007, the board released its first ever public business strategy: Five-2-Fifty. The ambition was to secure two premierships and 50,000 members in five years.

Considering the club had only so far won nine premierships in its over 100 years of existence, with its last over 16 years prior in 1991, and with the club's membership dwindling below 28,000 members, this strategy seemed ambitious to say the least.

In his autobiography *Relentless*, Sam Mitchell – the club's captain from 2008 to 2010 – wrote about the playing group's apprehension at such a lofty goal: 'When Jeff announced in 2007 the club's five-year Strategic Plan, it caught many people … including the playing group, by surprise. It seemed an outrageous statement at the time … We just had to get on with the job of somehow trying to make it come to fruition'.

In fact, professional sporting club boards had never been so public about their ambition. But Hawthorn finally had a purpose. Hawthorn Football Club President – the Hon Jeffrey G Kennett AC – was specific and clear with his language. His Senior Coach Alastair Clarkson, a former school teacher, was able to clearly couple the overall ambition of the club with his daily and weekly focus on winning the next game. Hawthorn CEO Ian Robson mobilised the administration staff so that their actions reflected their ambitions.

Momentum grew. The 28,000 members soon swelled to 32,000, then 35,000, 45,000 ... and then 55,000.

At the end of the five years the Hawthorn Football Club had swelled to 75,000 members, and were considered a powerhouse again despite only securing one premiership cup within that period, in 2008. However, the foundation for success had been set and the club won a further three premierships in 2013, 2014 and 2015.

What happened inside the club to deliver such a dramatic and public turnaround? While Five-2-Fifty provided a clear roadmap to success, how did the players and staff convert that strategy into such tangible results?

With Clarkson (aka Clarko) leading the charge, the club participated in a program known as Leading Teams. Leading Teams had been associated with AFL clubs for a number of years, and had been credited with helping Geelong to three premierships from 2007 to 2011. The program demanded that players, coaching and administration staff alike took an honest look at themselves, and confront the gaps between standards of behaviour they set and agreed on together and what actually happened, both on and off the field.

The program supported the group to establish a culture of feedback – where constructive feedback was both sought after and shared between players and coaching staff. Everyone, regardless of seniority or status, had an equal role to play in meeting the standards set by the group; no-one was exempt. The principles and practices established in that program were reinforced through daily habits and behaviours, led by the players and supported throughout the rest of the culture.

I interviewed Brad Sewell, a key senior player for the club and now an AFL commentator, during those pivotal years about his perspective on the Leading Teams experience. He said: 'It enabled the creation of positive conflict in a way that depersonalised feedback and criticism … it promoted a certain style of feedback, which was only to be constructive … whereby it wasn't about the individual, it was about the cause, it was about your role. It was bigger than any one person'.

Sewell explained that key to driving a high-performance environment at Hawthorn was normalising feedback as part of everyday conversation: 'The analogy was for this exercise not to become like church, where you would go to church on Sunday and profess all of your sins and beg for forgiveness, but that was the only time you checked in through that lens. The challenge was to create an environment whereby confronting conversations could be had in the hallway, could be had at the water cooler, could be had over a meal, could be had on a day-to-day basis. Whereby if those conversations were seen through the lens, they would make us better.'

While the program helped the group confront the brutal facts, it also helped leaders establish strong relationships that ensured difficult conversations would not damage trust and respect. In his book, Mitchell shared how he learned to adapt his signature forceful style: 'I became a more rounded, empathetic leader. I was a work in progress. The change was born out of a need to work more closely with my team mates, rather than pushing too hard against them the other way.'

The Hawthorn Football Club established a leadership system which went far beyond the performance of the team. It created a shared purpose for all stakeholders (players, staff and supporters alike), communicated it effectively and made it part of their community's DNA. They created a culture of accountability to leadership behaviours, both on and off the field, which saw the club re-emerge as a force in the AFL.

Understanding that leadership is a system of performance – a series of habits and behaviours that became established as part of the new culture – was the key factor that cemented Hawthorn Football Club's legacy.

5

The multiplying effect of good leadership

I love it when a compelling piece of research confirms what we intuitively know to be true. Research by Gallup showed that modern-day workers are primarily motivated by personal and professional development, and increasingly want to work with managers who coach, not bosses who tell.

Gallup published 'Building a High-Development Culture Through Your Employee Engagement Strategy' in 2019, sharing the results of a meta-analysis covering 1.8 million employees, 230 organisations and 49 industries in 73 countries.

What they found is that the relationship we have with our manager is still the most important one in the business; 70% of the variance in team engagement is determined solely by the manager.

More importantly, managers who adopt a coaching mindset and focus on developing their people deliver the strongest engagement and performance results, including 41% lower absenteeism, 20% higher sales, and 21% higher profitability.

And yet, managers who prioritise the development of their people are the exception, not the rule. Because still, after 50 years of Gallup research, only 15% of employees worldwide are engaged at work. Only 15% of the 1.8 million people surveyed! How much faster could we all be progressing our families, communities, economies and environment if that 15% was reversed to 85% worldwide?

In fact, Gallup says that 'if leaders could prioritise one action, it should be equipping their managers to become coaches. This means putting engagement front and centre as a primary role responsibility'.

In my experience working with hundreds of leaders across a wide range of industries, the reasons we continue to observe this large knowing/doing gap are that leaders:

- don't understand that coaching and developing the talents of their people is part of their job description

- think skill development is covered by the People and Culture department

- misconstrue 'coaching' as telling someone what to do

- have simply never been trained in how to coach or how coaching drives engagement and performance.

The Gallup findings are further supported by Gartner research on the top five priorities for Human Resources (HR) leaders in 2020. Building critical skills and competence was listed as the number one priority in supporting business growth and improving operational excellence. The report stated that only one in five employees say they have the skills necessary for their current toles and future careers, and 70% say they haven't even mastered the skills they need for their jobs today.

While HR and other executives state this as their greatest priority, bridging the skills gap comes down to what people leaders do. HR teams partner with leaders to provide the tools, systems, content, access and opportunities that foster employee learning and growth. But it's the daily conversations that happen between leaders and their teams that embed learning and foster skills acquisition.

To bridge the skills gap, the Gartner report recommends that people leaders:

- challenge employees to be *more* – demonstrate how they will grow personally from in-demand skills (aka – ramp up the *challenge*)

- take a market-driven predictive approach to identifying skill needs by connecting employees to the market

- connect employees to skill-building opportunities beyond their roles by brokering learning opportunities internally and externally (aka – ramp up people's *capacity*).

Leaders hire people. Leaders develop people. Leaders connect people to purpose and broker the opportunities and experiences that develop critical job skills.

> **Helping leaders understand their role in setting clear benchmarks for performance, coaching and giving feedback, and holding them accountable to these behaviours, is mission critical to workplace engagement and performance.**

THE LEADERSHIP LADDER

The leadership ladder describes styles of leadership ranging from hostile leadership to inspiring leadership. A leader's behavioural style determines what they focus on when dealing with people, and impacts the effectiveness of their time investment – their 'effort-to-result ratio'. The effort-to-result ratio is how much time a leader puts in with their people versus the results generated from that time investment.

Liz Wiseman, author of *Multipliers: How the best leaders make everyone smarter*, talks about two types of leaders:

- Leaders who drain intelligence, kill ideas and sap energy. These are the diminishers of talent.

- Leaders who amplify the smarts and capabilities of people around them. Who inspire employees to stretch themselves to deliver results that surpass expectations. These are the multipliers of talent.

I agree with Liz, *and* I think that the best leaders do more than just multiply talent.

They transform potential.

Like enzymes that act as catalysts for chemical transformations, inspiring leaders activate potential by leveraging talent in the pursuit of shared purpose.

And unlike diminishers who tend to soak up all the attention in a room and insert themselves into every decision, inspiring leaders make a big impact with less effort.

The leadership ladder

Leadership	Focus on	Behaviour	Effort-to-result ratio
Inspiring	Potential	Visionary	1:10
Supportive	People	Ask oriented	1:5
Directive	Results	Tell oriented	1:1
Busy	Action	Task oriented	5:1
Hostile	Control	Dictator	10:1

Let's have a look at each of these, starting from the bottom up.

Hostile leaders

Hostile leaders are like **dictators** who rule by command and **control** because it makes them feel safe. People working with hostile leaders are too afraid to think for themselves or step outside the box, even if they know a smarter, more efficient way of doing things. It's safer to shut up and do as you're told. These leaders micromanage every task, putting in 10× the effort to produce a result. This style is actually a business liability in lost productivity, turnover, disengagement, sick leave and even fair work claims. The hostile leader's mantra is 'just get it done'. They see people as a commodity and just need to see action.

Busy leaders

In contrast to hostile leaders, **busy** leaders are absent. They're focused on **action** and are **task oriented** – they are just too busy to get to you. They prioritise their customers, their superiors, their own task lists, before you. If you're a member of their team, your meetings get bumped, interrupted, or they just don't happen. This style is also ineffective because busy leaders are underestimating the talent in their teams, holding onto too much work, not delegating enough, and not gaining value from the people they have. Their effort-to-result ratio is more like a 5:1 ... they put in 5× the effort to produce a result. The busy leader's mantra is 'I'm busy'. They prioritise their workloads and haven't yet keyed into the latent potential around them.

Directive leaders

Directive leaders are **results** focused and **tell oriented**. They keep their eyes on the results necessary to achieve high standards and direct people by telling them what to do. If you produce results, you're slapped on the back. If you fail to produce results, you're just slapped! Directive leaders achieve a 1:1 ratio of effort to results. They are very capable at delivering a positive profit and loss report, but are quick to burn people out. While they may deliver returns, they incur hidden costs through sick leave and turnover. The directive leader's mantra is 'show me the money'. They care about results, and the most definitive measure of results in business is cash.

Supportive leaders

Supportive leaders focus on **people** and are **ask oriented**. They prioritise people over results. They understand that an investment in people is an investment in the business. They spend time coaching and developing capabilities, asking questions to activate creative intelligence, and instil confidence in others. Supportive leaders have more engaged teams and gain better results for their efforts. For every hour they invest in people, they get 5× the result. The supportive leaders mantra is 'I care'. They care about the happiness and health of their people, and this translates into sustained return on investment.

Inspiring leaders

Inspiring leaders go one step further than supportive leaders – inspiring leaders are **visionaries**. They are not just focused on who you are – but on who you have the **potential** to be. These leaders share purpose and ignite passion. They are so clear on their vision that it becomes impossible *not* to get excited by it. For these leaders, we're capable of producing extraordinary results over sustained periods without burning out.

> **Inspiring leaders achieve a 1:10 effort to result ratio; they are light touch, with big impact.**

An hour a week, sometimes just an hour a month, is all we need to stay focused, aligned, productive, engaged and innovative with these leaders. The inspiring leader's mantra is 'I believe'. They believe in potential and the possibility of who we can become.

In his seminal work *Start with Why*, Simon Sinek says that great leaders inspire people to act: 'Those who are able to inspire will create a following of people – supporters, voters, customers, workers – who act for the good of the whole not because they have to, but because they want to.'

***

Along your journey, have you worked for an inspiring leader? What did it do for your creative intelligence? Your energy? Your ability to deliver sustained periods of high performance? What did it do for your career? Your happiness? Your health?

Jim Collins is the bestselling author of *Built to Last* and *Good to Great*. He defines leadership as 'the art of getting people to do what must be done'.

In reality, the leadership ladder describes styles that all leaders adopt at different points to motivate people to do the work that must be done. But leaders who anchor their style in supporting and inspiring their people produce the most remarkable results through their teams. They are the leaders who transform potential. If you're a leader, the question you need to be asking yourself is, where do you spend the balance of your time across these styles of leadership? And if you're overinvesting in the styles that take more effort with less result, perhaps it's time for you to adopt The Leadership System.

6

Introducing
The Leadership System

The Leadership System is a perpetual process of building capability in your people and inspiring high performance in the service of the organisation's purpose. The system is a series of deceptively simple behavioural codes for unlocking performance through leadership. The only trick is mastering these codes as part of your leadership DNA and applying them consistently over time.

THE THREE ELEMENTS OF THE LEADERSHIP SYSTEM

We are not born with these codes downloaded – leadership is a *learned* skill. How your team performs comes down to how you're leading them:

- If you want to inspire your team to reach aspirational goals – set clear **standards**.

- If you want your team to be more accountable – normalise giving and receiving **feedback**.

- If you want your team to continuously improve – coach and develop their **strengths**.

Let's have a look at each of these.

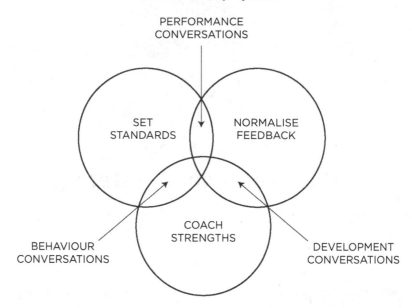

The Leadership System

Set standards

Means exactly that – setting measurable benchmarks for performance that reflect the shared purpose and values of the organisation. High-performing teams set high standards for themselves and each other – they reach for stretch goals and targets that keep them working to their performance edge – the place where performance meets potential – where learning and growth occurs as a natural part of the performance process.

Normalise feedback

Leaders who drive high-performing teams never miss an opportunity to reinforce positive results with positive feedback. In high-performing teams, feedback is seen as a gift because not only does it contribute to learning, it deepens trust and respect. In high-performing teams, feedback is normalised as a behaviour that is essential to meeting agreed standards. Feedback is both given well and received well because it's heavily weighted towards recognising positive effort and sharpening the application of strengths. When we normalises feedback, we create cultures where people are receptive to holding themselves and others accountable to results.

Coach strengths

Coaches adopt an 'ask, don't tell' mentality to activate the innate intelligence and creative problem-solving capabilities of their teams. They seek and appreciate individual strengths and put these strengths to work in helping people maintain their energy in the achievement of stretch goals. Leaders who ask are talent activators – they ask people to bring their best game and empower them to own their decisions, behaviours and ultimately their own results.

THE INTERSECTIONS

Powerful conversations are the glue that ties the entire system together.

Performance conversations

When we set standards and normalise feedback, we are having performance conversations. We are objectively assessing whether people are meeting pre-set goals and standards. Individuals and teams shouldn't be left wondering how they are performing or how the business overall is performing. Objective, measurable data on performance needs to be easily accessible, communicated through the right channels, and discussed between managers and their teams.

Development conversations

When we normalise feedback and coach strengths, we are having development conversations. We identify the development actions that enable ongoing learning and development in the role and support sustained high performance. Development conversations result in development plans aimed at fast-tracking an employee's professional and career progression. These plans are clear signals that a manager is actively seeking mutually beneficial outcomes both for the business and for their people.

Behaviour conversations

When we coach strengths and set standards – we are having behaviour conversations. We highlight the behaviours that align with our organisational values and support achievement of our performance standards. Behaviour conversations are crucial to reinforcing that the company values are not just words on a website – they are standards that we live by and measure ourselves against because we know that these behaviours ultimately deliver the best outcomes for the business in the long term.

* * *

> **When leaders continually set standards, normalise feedback, and coach strengths, they enable their people to quickly move through cycles of growth and amplify performance in a structured and supported way.**

This is good for them and it's good for the business.

Leaders who learn and systematically apply these behaviours create cultures of psychological safety, where it's safe to set and hold each other accountable to high standards in the shared interests of the individual, and the business.

HOW THE LEADERSHIP SYSTEM FUELS PURPOSE

At the age of 22, my partner (now husband) and I, after having been together for all of three months, decided to travel by bicycle and tent through Spain and Morocco. We saved every dollar, bought all the equipment, and after six months of planning, said goodbye to our jobs and homes in Melbourne to set out on our big adventure. We landed in Barcelona, pulled the bikes together and finally set off.

Up until that point I hadn't anticipated how tough it was going to be. It was December in Spain; bloody cold. Rain and wind battered us on our first day. After our first 20km, with another 60km to go to our destination for the night, I was already off the bike, throwing a tantrum, wishing I could dump the whole disastrous idea and jump on the next passing Contiki bus.

Clinton was frustrated with me … yes … but managing it. He didn't let me get away with being small then, and he still doesn't now. Clinton got off his bike and reminded me why we were there. He held my face and told me we are in this to have a real adventure together. He didn't know any other woman brave enough to even suggest this crazy idea, let alone follow through with it. And besides, if we kept going, I was going to get a really sexy bum! That clinched it. I drew a deep breath, and got back on that bike. And, while it was still physically, mentally and emotionally challenging every single day for the next six months, we were indeed having the adventure of our lives. I'd never felt more free.

There are still moments I reflect back on that bike ride – the orange groves of Valencia, the endless desert of the Sahara, the majestic gates of Fez. I remember what it felt like to have clear purpose and to let that carry me like a strong wind at my back.

The road to high performance is bound to be a bumpy ride. High performers have high expectations of themselves and others. They see mountains to climb and set out for the summit. But just like climbing a real mountain – it's bloody hard. It takes grit. Perseverance. Sacrifice. It's uncomfortable. And unless there's someone pointing to the top and telling us all how good the view is going to be up there, how proud we will feel and how strong we will become, it's easy to throw down the backpack and blame them for insisting on climbing this stupid mountain in the first place.

Leaders are custodians of purpose.

By working with The Leadership System, leaders foster the dynamic capabilities that keep people connected to the organisation's purpose and build both resilience and resourcefulness in our rapidly changing and dynamic world.

'Motivating people by articulating a compelling purpose is a well-established leadership task. Leaders who remind people of why what they do matters – for customers, for the world – help create the energy that carries them through challenging moments,' writes Professor Amy Edmondson in *The Fearless Organization*.

Getting to the top of the mountain is worth it – it builds confidence, self-worth, self-assurance, a sense of purpose and meaning in one's life, greater resilience, and a healthy mental state. But nothing worth achieving comes easy. The only thing that pulls us through is being clear on the purpose, the reason, the *why* behind it.

The Leadership System is a process for making sure the purpose becomes the language and the actions of the business and the people within it.

7

The importance of clear standards

Setting standards is about being clear on the outcomes for performance; but not being prescriptive about how to get there. It's about pointing the direction you want people to go; but letting them navigate their own path. This can at first seem paradoxical. How can you exert control as a leader over an outcome without controlling the way that outcome is achieved?

In *First, Break All the Rules*, Marcus Buckingham and Curt Coffman discuss this dilemma that many leaders and managers face; the dilemma of needing to deliver performance without controlling how people get there. The solution they say is 'define the right outcomes and then let each person find his own route toward those outcomes'. To create high performance, it is necessary to expect high standards. But allowing people the opportunity to find what Buckingham refers to as 'their path of least resistance' creates an environment that excites talented people to learn, grow and improve in the achievement of set standards.

As part of the research for this book I interviewed Jamie Cook, one of three founding partners for Stone & Wood Brewing Company, first introduced in part I. Stone & Wood is a privately owned beer brewer, based in northern New South Wales.

When I asked Jamie about how he and his co-founders inspired high performance, he communicated the importance of starting with a clear purpose.

> *So very early days, when we developed our purpose statement, which was very much around establishing a sustainable brewing business that develops, embraces and adds value to its communities, and that being all of the communities surrounding the business … so the team, suppliers, customers, drinkers, shareholders, community, and the environment. We go to work every day to try and add value to all of those communities. So people are focused not just on performing, but on adding value and creating value in those relationships.*

In terms of maintaining high performance, Jamie also stressed the importance of setting high benchmarks:

> *In terms of performance and people making sure they're on mission or on target, I guess you've got to be a little bit of an attention to detail freak and set high standards. I've had feedback over the years, you're a tough taskmaster or you set high standards, but at the end of the day, if you don't do that, then you don't create a great business, in my view. So yeah, just good enough isn't good enough. And I think people have that same perspective in the business.*

For standards to be effective, we must both role model the standards expected and explain them in clear, measurable terms.

FOUR STEPS TO SETTING STANDARDS

1. **Remember that people are not mind readers.** They cannot tell what your expectations are simply by reading your facial expressions. Yet many leaders assume that their people should just 'get it'. They often delegate tasks or set new projects; but miss the part where they explain the standard of work they expect. Communicate your expectations clearly and often. Repetition is good!

2. **Stick to measurable objectives that deliver results.** Generic statements, metaphors, and riddles are not standards. For standards to be effective, they must be motivating, aspirational, positively worded, and above all – measurable.

3. **Role model your standards.** Remember the old 'do as I say, not as it do' adage? It doesn't work. You can't have a two-class system. Leaders must hold themselves accountable to the same standards as everyone else. Otherwise they are just empty statements. And by the way – it's OK to slip up. You're only human. It's how you acknowledge your own slips and demonstrate your own vulnerabilities and learning styles that matters. Openly recognise your own mistakes and move on.

4. **Communicate WHY something is important.** Your people need to know how their roles make an impact on customers, the team, and the business. They need to know how what you're asking them to do enables performance. Many leaders fall short in doing the work of translation – translating how individual actions drive results. Make the link clear for people – and if that means being more transparent with your numbers – then embrace it. Educate your team on the business of the business and help them understand how to read the metrics that matter by trusting them and sharing your numbers.

MAKE YOUR STANDARDS MOTIVATING

For standards to be motivating, they need to be less about compliance and more about opportunities for excellence.

> **Humans are teleological in nature – we have an innate tendency to move towards a goal.**

Setting and achieving goals are well-researched contributors to psychological health and mental wellbeing.

Self-determination theory is a theory of motivation and personality developed by Richard Ryan and Edward Deci which identifies three fundamental psychological needs that allow for optimal function and growth:

1. The need for **competence** – the need to be effective in dealing with our environment.

2. The need for **relatedness** – the need for connectedness and relationships with others.

3. The need for **autonomy** – the need for personal control over one's own life.

We naturally seek challenging opportunities and thrive off a sense of independence while also feeling connected within a social group. Daniel Pink more recently re-positioned these needs as the innate human tendency for *autonomy*, *mastery* and *purpose*.

This is important for leaders to consider when they are setting standards and expectations for performance. There is a need for balance in organisational systems to allow for these basic human needs to be met. For leaders, this is relevant in working to design strategies, job roles, organisational structures and feedback mechanisms. The strategy must align the team, and job roles must be clear about who is accountable for what so that it's clear to see how achievement depends on teamwork, but each individual must demonstrate personal achievement and mastery within their role for the whole system to work well.

REVISITING SMART

Now we're all familiar with the SMART acronym for goal setting; making goals specific, measurable, achievable, realistic and timeframed. But many of us have perhaps become a bit laissez-faire about implementing this approach, let alone considering whether it could be tweaked to better support our team's motivation.

Set measurable goals

Each person on your team needs a tailored set of measurable performance goals and KPIs. If goals are not measurable, how will your people celebrate achievement or be motivated to push harder? A simple way to test this is to ask yourself when you've written a goal – how will I know if I'm achieving it? Setting concrete and measurable goals eliminates the possibility of misunderstandings or misinterpretations of what high performance looks like.

Making goals measurable ensures we are paying attention to the right things. Measurable goals are quantifiable – they represent a number of some kind, 'a count, a total or sum, an average, a percentage, or a ratio', as described by Stacey Barr in *Prove It!* Measures keep us honest and accountable to our goals.

Set stretch goals

High-performing teams don't just want to beat the competition – they want to set new aspirational standards. They dream of what's possible and thrive on beating the odds.

Setting an 'achievable' goal is like asking an Olympian athlete to train for four years just to match the current world record. If you want extraordinary performance, inspire your team to reach beyond the status quo. Change the 'A' in 'SMART' and encourage your team to set *aspirational* goals.

Just like the aforementioned Hawthorn Football Club's Five-2-Fifty goal seemed initially out of reach to the playing group, having a new aspirational standard served to motivate the team to dream beyond what they currently thought possible. It demanded wholesale change to their culture and leadership style. While they did not achieve all of the goals laid out in their strategy within the first five years; they laid the foundation for success with premierships in three subsequent years. They put in place the quantifiable habits and practices that they knew would lead them to success and were not deterred – in fact, they became hungrier for the win and this spurred them on.

Achieving big things means having big goals and knowing what habits ultimately lead to success.

Set positive goals

Positively oriented goals are more powerful than negatively oriented goals. In *Positive Psychology Coaching*, Robert Biswas-Diener and Ben Dean help us understand that not all goals are created equal. In fact, goals that lead to greater levels of happiness and wellbeing are distinct from other goals by their:

- orientation
- content
- motivation.

Goal orientation

A positively oriented goal that represents achievement of a gain is a more powerful motivator than a negatively oriented goal that represents avoidance of a loss.

> **We are more likely to experience success when we set positively oriented goals – goals that deliver a positive outcome for ourselves or others.**

This is known as an 'approach goal'. On the flipside, we are less motivated by goals that represent the avoidance of a loss.

The key here is that the *same goal* can be worded as an approach or avoidance goal – but goals motivated by approach are more likely to be sustained than those motivated by avoidance. For this reason, we should aim to set positive goals that help us clearly see what is to be gained, not avoided.

Goal content

Goals that are about greater intimacy, generativity and spirituality create more happiness than goals related to power or position.

Goal motivation

Similarly, goals that satisfy intrinsic motivations such as happiness, wellbeing, autonomy, mastery or purpose deliver greater wellbeing benefits than goals that are motivated by extrinsic factors like wealth or status.

***

What research tells is that deep down, we are not motivated by money – but we are motivated by what money represents. Ultimately, wealth represents freedom – freedom to make choices and do the things we most desire, things that make our lives and the lives of others better. Asking ourselves what we're really motivated by – what the money represents to us – allows us to cut through to what is really important and to set goals that align with the attainment of intrinsically satisfying outcomes. Standards are motivators for performance.

Ultimately, people seek companies with aspirational standards for themselves and others; where they put themselves to the test and may be rewarded with the kind of success that generates greater freedom, choice and opportunity.

8

Using feedback to boost performance

Once standards for performance are clear and agreed to, people need to know how they are performing against those standards. Feedback is essential to performance.

Without it we are flying blind.

We've all heard the saying that 'no news is good news', but when it comes to inspiring high performance, it's just not true. In high-performance cultures and high-performing teams, leaders adopt a constant and daily habit of asking for and giving feedback, reinforcing the behaviours of their people that add value and bring us closer to meeting set standards.

> High-performing teams focus on highlighting good news – what people are *doing* that is effective and how those behaviours impact results.

Giving feedback on performance, talking about what works and what doesn't work, and creating a culture where it's safe to do so is a key link in The Leadership System chain.

CHANGING YOUR RELATIONSHIP WITH FEEDBACK

I used to dread feedback. I was afraid of it because I had a fear of failure, so I did everything I could to avoid it. My fear of failure made me a high achiever, yes, but it was energy sapping. Thankfully, my relationship to feedback started to change when I joined management consulting company Nous Group. Nous was the place I aspired to be after university. It was my professional goal. Being accepted as a consultant there was a big deal for me, and the experiences and learnings I gained set me up for a lifetime of performance consulting.

In my early days at Nous I attended a client meeting with one of the principals, Penelope. I took copious notes during the meeting and observed Penelope in action, keen to learn as much as I could. As soon as the doors on the lift closed on our way out, Penelope turned to me and asked, 'How do you think that went?' I was effusive in my praise. Then she said, 'Great, thank you. Now can I please have some feedback on what I could have done better?' I hesitated – clearly at a loss for words. Here was someone I respected, someone I was trying to impress, asking me to tell her where she'd fallen short. She could see I was struggling with it, so she gently asked again. 'There's always something I can do just a little better. What's something small, just the 1%?' This helped. I recalled that there was someone in the meeting who asked a question that Penelope only partly answered. She said, 'Oh yes, of course – I meant to answer her in two parts but I was distracted by my own train of thought. Thanks for pointing that out, that was helpful.' Whew … I'd done it! I started to relax, thinking the feedback conversation was over.

Then she turned to me and asked, 'Would *you* like some feedback?!' Yikes! Here it was, the very thing I'd been dreading. She said, 'I noticed you took lots of notes, but didn't offer any ideas in the meeting today. Steph, we hired you for your mind. I've seen you back in the office, and you've always got valuable things to add. Next time, I'd love to hear what you have to say, and I'm sure the client would, too.'

Penelope's words really stuck with me. She was appreciating what I had to offer and encouraging me to live up to my potential. I instantly knew I could trust her to be honest with me and let me know whether I was meeting the standards that she, and our clients, expected.

I later learned that this practice of asking for and giving each other feedback following every client interaction was not only encouraged, but expected at Nous. It was normalised to have an objective conversation about what we did well, and where we could have done better, each time we left a client meeting. At Nous Group, I re-learned my response to feedback. It went from something I dreaded for the possible shame of something not good enough being highlighted to something I enjoyed for the opportunity to learn or be appreciated. I learned how feedback, done well, deepens trust and respect. It creates safety in relationships that enables both parties to continuously learn and improve.

GETTING FEEDBACK RIGHT

Georgia Murch, author of *Fixing Feedback*, tells us that cultures like Nous are high performing because of the presence of 'feedback flow' – where the push to give feedback is as strong as the pull to receive it. There is an oscillation to it, a natural rhythm that flows between people, between teams, horizontally, diagonally and vertically.

Unfortunately, very few organisations have cultures of feedback flow. They rely too heavily on formal performance review processes. Formal reviews are necessary to set individual performance and development goals aligned to the Strategic Plan of the business, but they alone do not drive performance.

> **Daily on-the-spot feedback conversations enable the constant adaptation and adjustment to high-performance standards.**

We avoid these daily feedback conversations for two reasons:

1. We get the *quality* of feedback wrong. We give it badly, making it about the person, not about the behaviour.

2. We get the *quantity* of feedback wrong. We focus on negative feedback – only dishing it out when something's wrong or not up to an expected standard.

Feedback then becomes a negative experience and one we typically avoid for fear of damaging a relationship or making things worse.

To fix feedback and change the way we feel about it in workplaces, we need to do two things: get the quality right, and the quantity right.

Get the quality right

We need to radically change the way we approach feedback and start seeing it for what it is: a gift. Unfortunately, feedback is more like a dirty word because many of us have made the mistake of confusing it with praise or criticism.

Don't get me wrong. Praise has a place in the world.

Praise sounds like 'well done', 'great work', or 'go team!' It's great for morale. It makes people feel good. But it can also make people feel patronised and it doesn't increase performance. At a game of football – would you expect the players to take their guidance from the cheer squad or the coach? The cheer squad may lift energy, yes, but the coach directs the gameplay and has a meaningful impact on performance.

Criticism, however, is a double whammy. Not only does criticism kill morale – it doesn't increase performance.

Praise and criticism are opinions. They're judgements we make – generalisations from which others must play guesswork. Neither point out in detail what was good, what was bad, or why.

This is where constructive feedback comes in. Constructive feedback can be positive or negative. It's *constructive* in that it is about *behaviour*, and not the person.

> Behaviours are the expressions of our thoughts and feelings, values and beliefs, and personalities. Behaviours are not *who* we are, they're *how* we are, and the beautiful thing about behaviour is that it can change.

Positive and negative constructive feedback has a greater impact on performance than praise and criticism. This idea was first presented in Max Landsberg's book *The Tao of Coaching*, and then extended by Georgia Murch in *Fixing Feedback*.

Positive constructive feedback is about a specific behaviour that has a favourable impact. It sounds like:

When you prepare agendas for our weekly WIPs, it's great because it means we effectively manage our meeting time. Thank you.

Negative constructive feedback is about a specific behaviour that has an undesirable impact. It sounds like:

When you turn up to our WIPs without an agenda, it's a challenge because we often miss important points that you can't help but distract me with later. Next time, can I ask that you prepare for our WIPs with a brief agenda?

Praise and criticism are subjective opinions. Positive and negative constructive feedback are objective, based on specific observable facts. The following table summarises the difference between these different types of feedback.

Positive	Negative
Constructive positive feedback	**Constructive negative feedback**
• Specific – about behaviour	• Specific – about behaviour
• Objective – observable fact	• Objective – observable fact
• About a standard that is met or exceeded	• About a standard that is not being met
Praise	**Criticism**
• Vague – about a generalisation	• Vague – about a generalisation
• Subjective – just opinion	• Subjective – just opinion
• About effort well done	• About an effort that needs improvement

Appreciating the difference between praise, criticism and constructive feedback can be nuanced.

For example, calling someone 'organised' is praise.

Appreciating that they effectively use their calendar and consistently meet deadlines is constructive.

Calling someone 'disorganised' is criticism.

Letting them know that for the last two weeks, they have missed timelines you both set is constructive.

When we take the time to give our colleagues constructive feedback – positive or negative – it truly is a gift. We all make faster gains when we highlight what people do well, and where we see opportunities for improvement.

Get the quantity right

Most of the time, we feel the need to give feedback when something goes wrong: when a performance standard is not met, or when we see an opportunity to improve. There is a deficit focus on our feedback.

This habit gives feedback a bad name. We've all heard those words … 'Can I give you some feedback?' and done an internal shudder. We'd all rather avoid than approach feedback, and this is because we all have the ratio wrong.

We need to adopt a radical change in our relationship with feedback, and this means establishing a habit of giving positive feedback more often than negative feedback. In short, we need to notice the good stuff more than we notice the bad.

Marcial Losada was a Chilean psychologist who worked with Emily Heaphy and Barbara Fredrickson in the early 2000s to establish the positivity ratio of high-performing teams. In their studies, he distinguished high-performance, medium-performance and low-performance teams based on three criteria: profitability, customer satisfaction ratings and 360-degree feedback ratings (ratings provided by managers, peers, direct reports, and sometimes customers). The study showed that in high-performing teams, positive feedback is given nearly *six times more* than negative feedback; that's a ratio of 6:1 positive to negative feedback. In low-performing teams, the ratio is more like one to one.

Let's stop to consider this. Thinking of all the feedback you have provided in the past week, what would you say your ratio is? Are you having six positive feedback conversations for every negative conversation? Most of us may think a one-to-one ratio is enough. It's not. To be high performing, we need to increase the amount of positive constructive feedback we are providing.

There are two major advantages to positive feedback.

- **Positive feedback builds the equity in a relationship.**
  Noticing and appreciating the efforts of your colleagues builds up enough equity, so that when it comes time to address negative performance, they are more likely to take your feedback for what it is – a gift.

- **Positive feedback cues people into the behaviours that drive results.** An *HBR* article by Jack Zenger and Joseph Folkman examined the 360-degree feedback among 50,000 leaders in their own database. They discovered that for those who started at between the 50th and 80th percentile, positive feedback enabled 62% of this group to improve a full 24 percentage points (to move from the 55th to the 79th percentile). They concluded that 'only positive feedback can motivate people to continue doing what they're doing well, and do it with more vigour, determination, and creativity'.

THE DOS AND DON'TS OF FEEDBACK

Do:
- Give positive constructive feedback *on average* five to six times more often than you would give negative constructive feedback.
- Give feedback on the spot, frequently (preferably daily).
- Give positive feedback in public, negative feedback in private.
- Give feedback to all colleagues – not just the people you manage. Notice when your peers and your boss demonstrate great work or great behaviour.
- Give negative feedback when you see inappropriate behaviour or if someone is failing to do what they should be doing as part of their role expectations.

- Nip poor performance it in the bud – don't save negative constructive feedback up for a formal performance review.

- Give feedback confidently and calmly. Don't make it a big deal – make it part of everyday conversation. Say it, ensure both parties understand the circumstances, and move on. Just another conversation.

- Assess whether the person is the right fit for the role if underperformance continues despite ongoing feedback and coaching.

Don't:

- Apply positivity ratios too literally, or your feedback efforts will appear disingenuous and not produce the desired effect.

- Give positive comments as a prelude to a negative comment. This is akin to using the SH!T sandwich – negative feedback disguised in a positive bun. It confuses the message. Keep positive and negative feedback conversations separate. The only exception to this rule is when you are conducting a formal performance review, in which case you are assessing overall performance over a longer period.

- Go in unprepared when you're delivering negative constructive feedback. Get the facts straight first.

- Attempt a negative feedback conversation when you are tired, angry or frustrated. Be calm and objective to maintain safety in the conversation.

HOW TO GIVE FEEDBACK USING THE AID MODEL

In my experience, the one thing most leaders and managers struggle with is actually having the feedback conversation and getting the words out simply, elegantly, without tripping over themselves or sounding unreasonably harsh.

Max Landsberg's AID Model for feedback is in my opinion the simplest and most effective tool available. Its simplicity makes it easier to recall in the moment you need it. AID is an acronym for:

- **A – Actions:** The behaviours that the person is doing well or poorly, under review.

- **I – Impact:** The effect these actions are having.

- **D – Desired outcome**: The ways in which the person could do things more effectively.

The following table is a tool I've created and use regularly to train leaders and managers in how to use the AID Model to give both positive and negative constructive feedback.

Using the AID Model to give feeback

	Positive constructive	Negative constructive
Ratio	6	1
Actions	**'When you … '** *State the benchmark behaviour.* E.g.: 'When you completed your report on time … '	**'When you … '** *State the behaviour falling short of benchmark.* E.g.: 'When you failed to complete your report on time … '
Impact	**'It's great because … '** *State the positive impact of that behaviour.* E.g.: 'It was great because it allowed me to update our CEO prior to her board meeting.'	**'It's a challenge because … '** *State the negative impact of that behaviour.* E.g.: 'It was a challenge because our CEO went into the board meeting uninformed about our team's results.'
Desired Outcomes	**'How can we keep this up?'** *Explore other ways we can leverage this great behaviour, or continuously improve it.* E.g.: 'How can we use this great time management to complete other reports on time?' *Or* just simply say: 'Thank you!'	**'Next time … it would be better if … '** *State what the benchmark is …* And, 'What are your thoughts?' E.g.: 'Next time, I need your report by the 15th, or at least a heads up two days before if you're not going to make that timeline. Thoughts?'

TRAINING YOUR TEAM TO GIVE USEFUL FEEDBACK

Giving constructive feedback is easy when you have the tools and a culture of psychological safety.

> Empowering yourself and your team with the skills to give and receive feedback builds trust and respect, and delivers measurable performance outcomes.

Adopting a common language and using a common tool for feedback is best done in teams so that everyone adopts the new behaviours together and gives each other permission to change. Let's look at how you can do this:

1. Get your team together and give them each copies of the AID feedback tool.

2. Draw a line down the middle of a flipchart pad or whiteboard.

3. Ask the group: 'What are all the positive behaviours we'd like to see more of?' List these on the left side of the flipchart. Examples are: 'entering tasks in Asana', 'showing up at Friday lunch and learn sessions', 'arriving at meetings on time'.

4. Then ask: 'What are the negative behaviours we'd like to see less of?' List these on the right side of the flipchart. Examples are: 'arriving five minutes late to meetings', 'not checking in on how I am', 'not providing agendas in meetings'.

5. In pairs, practise using AID to give feedback, first on all the negative behaviours, then on all the positive behaviours. Swap giving and receiving each time.

6. Each feedback conversation should only be about 10 to 20 seconds. This is supposed to be a light-hearted and rapidly moving activity – they are not 'real' feedback conversations, they are just a practice (although sometimes they feel very real!)

7. Debrief on how it felt to use the framework, and how it felt to receive the feedback. Gain consensus on how the team will integrate this process into their everyday conversations.

HOW TO RECEIVE FEEDBACK WELL

When I interviewed Brad Sewell, three-time AFL Premiership player, he shared that at Hawthorn Football Club (HFC) they depersonalised feedback by removing humour and making sure that the feedback was always coming from a position of making the team better:

> *The challenge goes both ways, whereby there's a skill in being able to provide feedback through those lenses but then also, some learnings had to be done by individuals to accept that feedback without getting defensive, without arguing the point. The conversation becomes about the misalignment perceived between your behaviour and the standards we'd set. If it's depersonalised, it's easy to have that conversation.*

At HFC, players knew they needed to get better at receiving feedback and seeing it as a genuine effort to improve the performance standards for the whole team. They learned how to treat it like every other drill they might perform on the ground – it was something to lean into, not run away from.

> **To create feedback flow, leaders need to role model how to ask for feedback, and how to receive it without being defensive.**

Just like Penelope in the example shared earlier, leaders create cultures where it is safe to give and receive feedback by showing how it's done. Here are my tips to asking for and receiving feedback:

- Ask for feedback on a specific situation, behaviour or context. For example, instead of asking, 'How did I go?', ask, 'How well did I communicate my central ideas in that meeting?'

- Avoid being defensive (unless you never want to receive feedback again!). Avoid saying things like, 'yes ... *but* ...'. The second you try to explain your reason for being the way you were, you are justifying your behaviour.

- Paraphrase what you've heard, using their language as much as possible (not your spin on their language): 'So what I'm hearing you say is that when I ... it has an impact on ... '

- Ask for specific examples, seek clarification where someone shares just their opinion or makes a generalisation about you (positive or negative): 'What did I do that made the meeting great?' or 'What did I do that appeared competitive?'

- Where there is a misalignment between your perception and their perception, seek to understand the gap. Recognise that their perception is their reality.

- Suggest what you could do differently next time and seek their input: 'Next time, would it be better if I ... ?'

- See the feedback for what it is: an effort to improve performance for the whole business or the team and a sign of both trust and respect.

- Thank the person for their gift of feedback – remember, it took time and effort for them to share.

Asking for feedback in this way achieves three outcomes:

1. You learn something important about how your behaviour impacts people and results.

2. You role model how to ask for and receive feedback.

3. You build safety, trust and respect in the relationship.

HOW TO CREATE FEEDBACK FLOW

At Hawthorn Football Club, after every match, every player gave their performance a score out of 10, and also received a score out of 10 from the head coach. Where misalignment occurred between a self-score and any other score – the player and coach would have a feedback conversation. This process was considered an assessment of their 'on-field' performance. In addition, the players also rated every other player on their demonstration of the club's values and behaviours at least twice each year. This was how they assessed 'off-field' performance.

Brad Sewell believes that this dual focus on both on-field and off-field performance was an important mechanism in authentically living the club's ethos: 'One of the really important acknowledgments of the group was that you can't live a certain lifestyle and then profess to be something else to the group. In terms of professionalism and lifestyle, you had to go hand in hand.'

The club created feedback flow by designing specific processes into their weekly and daily schedules that both necessitated and normalised feedback conversations.

These same processes can, and should, be adopted in workplaces. While annual performance reviews where teams receive ratings from managers are common, they are not enough. Feedback conversations need to happen both within teams and with team leaders.

THE FEEDBACK ROUNDING EXERCISE

To fast track your team's ability to get over the fear of feedback and experience it as positive and constructive, get your team together for regular, perhaps quarterly, **feedback rounding** exercises. This activity works best in teams, and also when everyone knows how to use the AID feedback process described earlier. Here's how it's done:

- Working in pairs, each team member will have a 10-minute 'round' with every other team member where they will share at least three pieces of positive constructive feedback to one piece of negative constructive feedback.

- Set the team up in rows of chairs facing each other, 'speed-dating' style.

- In each 10-minute round, each team member has five minutes to give the other their feedback.

- At the end of each round, find a new partner by asking the people in one row to move one seat to the right (the person on the end jumps up and moves to the start).

- Run a series of 10-minute rounds – up to 90 minutes (everyone tires a little at this point). If your team is large and you need more rounds, have a break and start again.

- Ensure everyone thanks their partner at the end of each round.

- Keep the energy light; play music, use a bell or sound to signal when rounds are finished.

- Conduct a debrief with the whole group asking how it felt to receive positive and negative constructive feedback.

- Ask each person to share with the whole group – what themes they picked up, what others see as their top three strengths, and what others see as their greatest opportunity for improvement.

- Capture this information on a flipchart and put it in a shared workspace (in the office or online) so that everyone can continue to appreciate strengths and support each other's development.

9

Become a talent activator and amplifier

COACHING TO ACTIVATE TALENT

Coaching closes the loop on our leadership system.

> If we successfully set standards for performance and give feedback on how we are tracking, coaching is the key lever that supports people to lift or sustain achievement.

Leaders who adopt a coaching approach are talent activators – they ask people to bring their best game and empower them to own their own results.

Coaching is one of the most important modes that leaders can adopt to activate the innate intelligence and creative problem-solving capabilities of their teams. Of all the strategies that leaders can choose – mentoring, training, managing, directing – coaching is known to have a significant impact on workplace performance.

The Institute of Coaching in the US, an affiliate of Harvard Medical School, cites that 80% of individuals who receive coaching report increased self-confidence, and over 70% benefit from improved work performance, better relationships and more effective communication skills. They also report that 86% of companies feel that they recouped the investment they made in coaching, plus more.

Let's take a look at how powerful coaching can be.

Lea Thorpe was my practice leader at Nous Group and an absolute master at coaching. Because of her experience and position as both a Principal and Practice Leader in the consultancy, Lea was often asked to lead large proposal response teams. There was one in particular, early in my career at Nous, that was pivotal for the business. If we were successful, it was going to be the largest project Nous had ever undertaken. It was an important government contract with a high opportunity for us to live our primary reason for being: positive influence.

I attended the proposal team kick-off meeting with several other consultants, and was expecting to sit and listen for an hour to what I was supposed to do. Instead, Lea started the meeting with a question: 'What problem is the client asking us to solve?'

She listened to all of our responses and ideas. She then followed up with another question: 'What capability do we have that will help the client solve these problems?' For the rest of that meeting, Lea just kept on asking questions. Each time she asked a question, she would sit back in her chair, listen, nod, take a little note, and then follow it up with another considered question. Everything about her approach that morning told us, without needing to use any words, that she believed in our ability to write a compelling proposal. She used questions to help us find our own ideas and answers, and instilled in us a high degree of confidence that *we had this!*

Our tender was successful, and that project gave us the opportunity to develop relationships, IP and experiences that spawned several years of work with the client and launched many careers within Nous. If I draw a tree with branches to map that success story right back to its beginning, it all started with Lea's first question in that first meeting.

DIRECTING VERSUS COACHING

Coaching is a distinct mode adopted by leaders. The table below highlights the differences between directing and coaching.

Directing	Coaching
Telling mode	Asking mode
Controlling	Supporting
Takes less time	Takes more time
Prevents learning	Fosters learning
Diminishes creativity and intelligence	Activates creativity and intelligence
Creates dependency	Creates accountability

While directing takes less time and delivers a 'quick fix' solution, it creates dependencies that keep people coming back for the answers to questions they are perfectly capable of finding themselves. Coaching may take more time upfront, but it pays back with compound interest when people learn their own methods to solve problems and make decisions, speeding up productivity in the long run and freeing the leader to focus on opportunities for growth, disruption or continuous improvement.

COACHING TO AMPLIFY STRENGTHS

The real power of coaching is amplified when leaders coach to strengths. Coaching to people's strengths is about taking the path of least resistance to best results.

Strengths are people's natural talents that have been finely honed over years of practice. Our strengths are the things we are naturally talented at and enjoy doing. By this definition, if you're good at something but don't enjoy doing it then it's not a strength. We are all born with talents – natural predispositions that are linked to our genetic makeup. But a talent is just latent potential until it becomes a strength.

Talent = Latent potential

Gallup says that:

Talent + Investment (practice, coaching, development) = Strength

> **Research shows that when we play to our strengths, we achieve far greater gains in performance than if we address our weaknesses.**

A comprehensive study of over 19,000 employees across 34 organisations published by the Corporate Leadership Council in 2002 showed that the purposeful application of strengths enhances performance by up to 36%. In contrast, emphasising weaknesses led to a 26.8% *decline* in performance.

In addition to enhancing performance, the purposeful amplification of strengths is also proven to correlate with greater authenticity, happiness, self-efficacy, fulfilment and psychological vitality (Govindji & Linley, 2007), and goal attainment (Linley et al. 2010).

Leaders who know and understand this will work with people to match them to roles that will allow them to leverage their unique combination of strengths. In *First, Break All the Rules*, Marcus Buckingham advises us to: 'Focus on each person's strengths and manage his weaknesses. Don't try to fix the weaknesses … instead, do everything you can to help each person cultivate his talents.'

This sentiment is put into practice by Jamie Cook and his leadership team at Stone & Wood Brewing Company. When I interviewed Jamie, he talked about finding someone's 'sweet spot':

If someone's not performing as well as they should, potentially it's because they're not actually into what they're doing. Sometimes people are high performing in a role, but they're actually not very happy. It's that whole piece around, some people get put into a role because this is one of their strengths, but it's not necessarily something that they get enjoyment out of. And that really is stressful for people. And then it shows in their behaviour. They might be high performing, but their behaviours are impacted by it. So it's making sure people are in their right sweet spot, where they perform well and they also enjoy it.

ARE YOUR PEOPLE USING THEIR STRENGTHS?

Gallup research reveals that very few of us are actually using our strengths and talents at work. Their *State of the Global Workplace* report provided the global aggregate of Gallup data collected in 2014, 2015 and 2016 across 155 countries. The report indicates that **just 15%** of employees worldwide are engaged in their job. Two-thirds are not engaged, and 18% are actively disengaged.

This means that on average, fewer than one-third of workers strongly agree with the statement 'at work, I have the opportunity to do what I do best every day'. In contrast, employees who use their strengths every day are six times more likely to be engaged at work, 8% more productive, and 15% less likely to quit their job than those who do not. Jim Clifton, Gallup Chairman and CEO, summarised that 'the current practice of management — which attempts to turn weaknesses into strengths — doesn't work. Moving to strengths-based workplaces will change global productivity and growth overnight'.

A strengths-based approach is one of the best opportunities we have to realise the enormous pool of latent potential that exists in every organisation. Adopting a strengths-based approach changes the focus of the leader from one of controlling or directing to one of supporting or inspiring.

To adopt a strengths-based approach to coaching, you need to do three things:

1. adopt the mindset of a coach

2. ask, don't tell

3. use silence.

Let's consider each of these.

Adopt the mindset of a coach

To effectively coach is to believe in human potential. It is to believe that all people have within them an innate desire to do well, relevant life experiences to draw on, and natural talents to draw on in order to achieve their goals. Your role when coaching is to tap into that intelligence; to discover your team members' existing resources – both internal (strengths, values, beliefs, knowledge and skills) and external (finances, relationships, systems and tools) – and help them leverage these to experience greater fulfilment and performance at work.

Tim Gallwey is a former tennis champion, well-known coach and author on coaching and leadership. Gallwey sums it up beautifully in his simple model:

$$P = p - i$$

where Performance (P) is the result of potential (p)
minus interference (i)

Simply, there are no weaknesses. There is only interference. The role of a coach is to remove interference so others may realise their potential and experience maximum performance.

Interference can come in many forms, including:

- unrealised strengths
- defensive thinking styles
- lack of skill
- lack of will
- unrealistic expectations
- lack of clarity on goals
- poor planning
- poor time management
- toxic relationships

- lack of access to physical resources such as money, property, appropriate tools or other people with specialist skills and knowledge.

This is by no means an exhaustive list, but just some of the more common barriers that stand in the way of exceptional performance.

Ask, don't tell

The coaching golden rule is to 'ask, don't tell'. Asking questions is the means by which we activate intelligence and empower others to discover their own solutions. As humans, we are far more likely to do something if we came up with the idea ourselves (or at least believe that we did!). Every time we feed someone an answer to a question, we rob them of their opportunity to learn.

Telling people what to do may sometimes be a quicker solution in a busy, fast-paced environment. But this is playing a zero-sum game. What we gain in the short term, we lose in the long run with the same types of questions coming at us over and over again. By telling rather than asking, we unwittingly create dependencies that ultimately engulf our precious time. Then we blame these same people for not taking enough initiative. Go figure!

The idea that being a leader sometimes means answering a question with a question is directly opposed to what we typically expect of leaders. This feels like: 'Being the experienced person here – aren't I supposed to look competent and capable? Aren't I supposed to have the answers to these questions and therefore answer them?'

No! Free yourself of the tyranny of knowledge! Allow yourself to look like the dumbest person in the room. Create the space for all that remarkable intelligence around you to surface.

It can be challenging to make the switch and stop directing people. What you don't want to create is dependency. What you do want to create is a team of fast learners – who are challenged to discover better ways of doing things. Then you get to look amazing because you have the brightest, most engaged, most promotable team in the business. Win–win!

Ask magic questions

So, how do you put this into practice? Of all the questions you can ask, there are two magic questions that will change the dynamic of your team from one of dependence to one of empowerment. If you take nothing else from this book – just take this little nugget:

*Magic question # 1: 'What do **you** think you can do?'*

*Magic question # 2: 'What **else?**' × 3*

One of my clients is an owner in a fittings and fixtures company. He came to one of my workshops on coaching and was then keen to apply my principles to his workplace. He decided to use the magic questions and start answering any question from his team with a question. When we caught up two weeks later, he couldn't believe the difference: 'Just by asking people more questions and "what else", I've noticed a difference to the level of engagement and accountability in the business. If people are told what to do, they have considerably less ownership over it.'

Here are some other types of questions you could ask:

- **Closed questions** end in a one-word answer. They can be used for checking on understanding. Closed questions often start with *when, where, do you, did you, have you, is* and *can.*

- **Open questions** require more than a one-word answer. These are the ideal questions to open up a coaching conversation, because they require the coachee to think. Open questions often start with *what, how* and *why.*

- **Probing questions** are used to go deeper on a particular line of inquiry. Examples are: 'So tell me more about why you want to move into a more senior role?', 'How will more responsibility make you feel?'

- **Leading questions** are used to lead someone to an intended outcome. Examples are: 'Why is looking after your family the most important thing to you?', 'How can you encourage this international office to speak more in English rather than Vietnamese?'

Start by asking, and build on it

A participant in a coaching workshop I was running recently asked me what they could do when confronted with a team member who clearly had a major skill gap in the area they were trying to coach them on.

When we've truly reached the edge of someone's understanding – and we're the subject matter expert in that area – do we remain a coaching purist and leave them hanging? Of course not! Coaching is simply a mode that leaders adopt. Sometimes it is appropriate to switch modes to training, mentoring, managing or directing.

In her book *Leaders Who Ask*, Corinne Armour makes this important distinction between people who coach for a living and leaders who adopt a coaching approach as one mode to develop their people:

1. The leader who asks retains some influence over the coaching focus.

2. The leader who asks may be a subject matter expert.

3. The leader who asks chooses when to coach and when not to.

In other words, it's appropriate to adapt your coaching approach depending on the level of knowledge, skill or experience your team member has.

In *The Tao of Coaching*, Max Landsberg wrote about a repertoire of response options along the 'ask versus tell' continuum:

1. Ask questions and paraphrase.

2. Suggest.

3. Demonstrate.

4. Give advice.

5. Tell what and how.

This is shown in the following diagram.

The 'ask versus tell' continuum

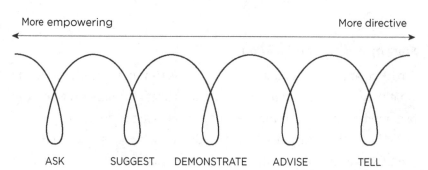

So, how can we tell when coaching is the right mode, and when to switch to other modes?

We start by asking; and build on it.

Explore what someone already knows. Find the edge of their knowledge and skill. Then, like adding layers to a cake, or building on an existing frame, strengthen their existing neural network by extending what they already know.

This is how a coaching conversation could move along the ask versus tell continuum:

1. Ask and explore fully: 'What options and ideas do you already have?', 'What else?'

2. Suggest: 'Can I suggest some options for you to consider?'

3. Demonstrate: 'Can I show you an option?'

4. Give advice: 'The option I would choose in this situation is … '

5. Tell what and how: 'The way I see it, your best option is to … '

In my experience, many leaders default straight to tell mode. It's a powerful impulse to supposedly help others and speed up our efforts by telling. But this mode slows down learning and innovation – two factors critical to growth. Starting by asking puts you in coach mode at least initially, and gives you the insight you need to build the capabilities of people around you.

Use silence

Listening is a core skill of coaching. This is one of the reasons why I love coaching so much. When you're coaching, you're actually doing very little of the real work; all you're doing is creating a space for the other person to do *their* work – the work of thinking through their own challenge or opportunity. Listening creates the space for others to follow their own thought process.

As a coach, when you ask a question, let it sit. Often, the other person won't have an immediate answer, especially if you've asked the magic question, 'What else?' If you've reached the edge of their understanding, they need to think. Silence opens up the space for thinking. In silence comes new thinking. It asks us to go beyond what we know and start reaching into our potential zone; exploring new possibilities.

We are not used to silence in conversations. Silence feels uncomfortable, so we rush to fill it to avoid discomfort. Be okay with silence. You are giving someone the gift of time and space to think – something that is rare and meaningful in our hectic, task-driven work lives.

There is a misconception that innovation is an energising, fun process that happens when people brainstorm and throw post-it notes on a wall. Sometimes innovation happens that way. But, most of the time innovation happens when people wrestle with the unknown. When people are willing to step into their vulnerability and admit they don't have the answers. When they're willing to suggest seemingly stupid ideas, to make random connections, to follow trains of thought and explore possibilities. Innovation is borne of trial and error.

> **Allowing silence in a coaching conversation gives space for innovation to seed.**

USE GROW FOR COACHING

There are many coaching models out there and they all have merit. The one I prefer to use myself and train leaders in is the GROW model, first introduced by Sir John Whitmore in his book *Coaching for Performance* in 1992. It has since gained massive popularity among professional coaches and the business community because of its simplicity.

GROW is an acronym for four stages of a coaching conversation.

G – Goal: 'What do you want to achieve?'

Start a coaching conversation by establishing the goal of the conversation. Get clear on what you and the other person need to walk away with for the conversation to be a useful investment of time. Sometimes it's appropriate for the coachee to set the goal of the conversation ('I need help understanding how to compose the board report'). Other times, it is appropriate for the coach or leader to set the goal of the conversation ('I'd like to help you come up with strategies to achieve your sales target this month'). Whoever sets the goal of the conversation – spend a moment getting clear on this at the start.

R – Reality: 'What is the situation?'

Understand the challenge or issue that needs to be resolved. Establish what the blockers are – the interference that is getting in the way of the person achieving their potential. Blockers can be real or imagined. They can be real people who are preventing access to necessary resources. They can be self-limiting beliefs or misunderstandings about role or purpose in role. They can be a real lack of skills or knowledge in an area. When exploring reality, spend time understanding how the coachee views the problem or issue; and what they've already tried to do. Resist the temptation to start problem solving here. Moving too hastily through this step will mean you scope limited options to the problem.

O – Options: 'What are your options?'

This is where the magic questions are asked: 'What do you think you can do?' Explore all the options – especially beyond the immediately obvious ones. Ask the question, 'What else?', *at least* three times. Allow the silence to sit while the person pushes their thinking in new ways. If you've reached the limit to the person's understanding and you are able to offer some options, start working your way down the 'ask versus tell' repertoire – suggest, demonstrate and give advice. The options stage is where you want to spend a majority of your time in a coaching conversation.

W – Way forward: What actions will you take?

Identify what they will go away and do from the conversation. Make these actions SMART – specific, measurable, aspirational, realistic, timeframed. Ask them what strengths they will leverage to achieve their goal. Ask them how they will activate the support they need – either support from you or support from colleagues around them.

The following diagram summarises your intention at each stage of the coaching conversation.

Your intention at each stage of the coaching conversation

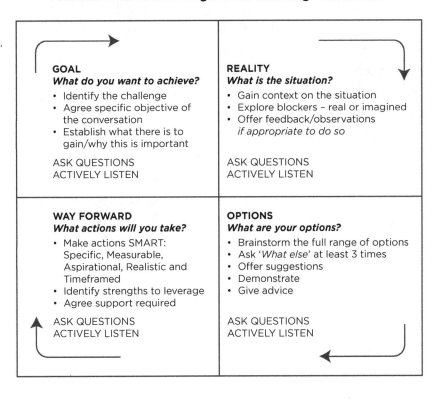

GOAL
What do you want to achieve?
- Identify the challenge
- Agree specific objective of the conversation
- Establish what there is to gain/why this is important

ASK QUESTIONS
ACTIVELY LISTEN

REALITY
What is the situation?
- Gain context on the situation
- Explore blockers – real or imagined
- Offer feedback/observations *if appropriate to do so*

ASK QUESTIONS
ACTIVELY LISTEN

WAY FORWARD
What actions will you take?
- Make actions SMART: Specific, Measurable, Aspirational, Realistic and Timeframed
- Identify strengths to leverage
- Agree support required

ASK QUESTIONS
ACTIVELY LISTEN

OPTIONS
What are your options?
- Brainstorm the full range of options
- Ask '*What else*' at least 3 times
- Offer suggestions
- Demonstrate
- Give advice

ASK QUESTIONS
ACTIVELY LISTEN

GROW can be used in many formats and contexts:

- from short, five-minute interactions to hour-long meetings

- coaching individuals or teams

- managing customer enquiries or dealing with customer complaints

- for sales conversations (where your product or service is the way forward)

- for problem-solving or brainstorming workshops

- for managing conflicts or negotiating.

Coaching is our process for helping people find their path of least resistance towards high standards of performance. Coaching is distinctly different from telling people how to do their jobs – a quick path to disempowering people or creating unnecessary dependencies that impedes the progress and performance of the whole team. To coach is to believe in the inherent potential and talent that exists within every human being. The role of the coach is to remove barriers to performance and help others leverage their strengths in roles they are naturally good at and enjoy doing.

As you will see in the next chapter, making these conversations regular brings the whole system together. Jamie Cook from Stone & Wood Brewing Company is a believer in regular powerful conversations: 'At the end of the day, if you're enabling your team, you've got to make sure they're developing throughout the year and not just one opportunity at feedback.'

10

Have powerful conversations

Having the right conversations in the right way and at the right time is a learned skill. This chapter provides leaders with all the tools they need to nail these conversations and help employees and their business flourish.

PERFORMANCE CONVERSATIONS

Performance conversations are where standards and feedback intersect. When we have performance conversations, we objectively assess whether people meet pre-set goals and standards that are clearly linked to the company goals.

This is why it's so important to set measurable goals and standards that are relevant to the role and aligned to overarching company goals. We need to be able to objectively say whether something was achieved or not achieved; and to clearly indicate how this role adds value within the organisation.

If performance standards are not achieved, there are a number of possible reasons why:

- performance expectations are unachievable and need to be recalibrated

- the person is still learning and needs more training

- the role is getting too big and needs to be rescoped; which may result in promotions, new hires, or a scaling down of responsibilities.

If, despite these supports and considerations, underperformance continues, formal disciplinary procedures need to commence. In *Traction*, Gino Wickman talks about a 'three-strike' rule:

- **Strike 1:** Discuss the standards and expectations required in the role and give the person time to correct (a period of two to four weeks is usually acceptable).

- **Strike 2:** If there is no improvement, discuss standards again and give them another two to four weeks to correct.

- **Strike 3:** If there is still no improvement, it is unlikely that they are going to change. In this case, for their own wellbeing (and the wellbeing of business) they must either be moved into a different role or moved out of the organisation with their dignity intact.

> **In cases where people do not achieve performance standards despite coaching and feedback, it is likely they are in a role that does not play to their strengths.**

If this is the case, feedback will be geared towards negative constructive, coaching will deliver only marginal improvements, and they will struggle to experience sustained job satisfaction. This is a fast-track lane to mediocre or poor performance. The most constructive thing you can do is help them find a new role – either in your organisation or elsewhere – that plays to their strengths and gives them more joy.

Conversely, when people are in roles that play to their strengths, feedback will be geared towards positive constructive, coaching delivers improvement, and they will experience far greater levels of job satisfaction.

Getting the right person in the right role is what my old boss used to call getting 'aces in their places'.

DEVELOPMENT CONVERSATIONS

Development conversations are where feedback and coaching intersect. When we have development conversations, we identify development goals and actions that enable ongoing learning and career development. Development conversations between leaders and their teams should be regular and formalised. Leaders who take a proactive approach to the development of their people signal that they care about more than just standards of performance, but also about development and growth of their people.

Meeting development goals need not be costly or time consuming. While formal training is important, most learning occurs on the job. The 70/20/10 model for learning was created by Michael Lombardo and Robert Eichinger to demonstrate that only 10% of learning comes from formal learning interventions, 20% from working with others, and a whopping 70% of learning comes from on-the-job experiences. Well-considered development goals and actions deliver benefits both to individuals and to the organisation:

For example:

- For someone whose goal is to deliver their sales budget for the quarter, a learning action may be to develop a call cycle plan.

- For someone whose goal is to launch a new range of muesli, a learning action may be to produce a market and competitor report.

- For someone whose goal is to implement a new customer service response system, a learning action may be to research all the current systems in the market and provide a recommendation.

- For someone whose goal is to prepare the monthly board report, a learning action may be to shadow their executive in a board meeting and discuss their insights afterwards.

- For someone whose goal is to improve the customer satisfaction rating, a learning action may be to respond to customer complaints and develop a response procedure for certain categories of complaints.

By making these connections in development conversations, leaders signal to their people that the extra effort and work they put into the achievement of goals are actually learning experiences that will benefit both their performance and career progression. Learning becomes part of every day, rather than something we do periodically in formal training. We are also giving people permission to play at new tasks, to make mistakes and learn from them in a safe way, before new responsibilities become a core part of their role. Instilling a developmental mindset supports the process of keeping people at their performance edge.

BEHAVIOUR CONVERSATIONS

Behaviour conversations are where coaching and standards intersect. When we have behaviour conversations, we highlight the behaviours that align with our organisational values and support achievement of our performance standards.

If performance conversations are about the *what*, behaviour conversations are about the *how*. They are about the small things that people do every day that either support or erode a positive and productive team environment.

For example, if you have *integrity* as a company value, having a behaviour conversation means appreciating times where people:

- worked overtime to solve a customer issue

- owned up to a mistake that cost the company time and money

- held themselves accountable to a target

- challenged others on taking shortcuts that would negatively impact quality or service

- made a business decision by using company values as a criteria

- said no to an opportunity that was not aligned with the company values.

To have effective behaviour conversations, it's important that you first have a tool to measure behaviour by. This is where having a clear set of values and behaviours is helpful. What does it look like and not look like to live the company values of integrity, customer focus, respect, innovation or leadership? Having a list of behaviours that provides examples of lived values helps remove the subjectivity of these conversations. (You can read about values and behaviours in chapter 15.)

Having regular behaviour conversations signals to your people that you value achievement and company performance, but not at the cost of your values. There is no point having a set of company values unless you hold yourself and others accountable to them. Without behaviour conversations, values lose their significance and become empty words.

11

Where leaders often go wrong

By fully embracing The Leadership System, leaders arm themselves with the tools to avoid the common traps that other leaders fall into. I've observed these pitfalls and even experienced them myself through the hundreds of hours coaching CEOs, executives and team leaders on how to get the best from their teams.

The way I see it, there are four common pitfalls where leaders work against themselves and unwittingly enable low or mediocre performance:

1. We don't give enough attention to our best people.

2. We're not addressing underperformance quickly enough, and this lowers the standard for everyone.

3. We invest time generating great Strategic Plans but fail at implementation.

4. We promote people with strong technical skills into leadership positions and forget that leadership, like any skill, is learned.

Let's take a closer look at these.

WE DON'T GIVE ENOUGH ATTENTION TO OUR BEST PEOPLE

We spend 80% of our time working with the 20% who are under-performing, when it should be the other way around.

The idea that many of us have our priorities wrong was presented by Marcus Buckingham and Curt Coffman in *First, Break All the Rules*:

> *If you pay the most attention to your strugglers and ignore your stars, you can inadvertently alter the behaviours of your stars. Guided by your apparent indifference, your stars may start to do less of what made them stars in the first place and more of other kinds of behaviours that might net them some kind of reaction from you, good or bad.*

If we're not paying enough attention to our top performers, we're actually rewarding average performance and ultimately stunting business growth. A study published in *Personnel Psychology* in 2013, which cut across several industries, revealed that the top 5% of the workforce at the researched firms produced 26% of the firm's total output. That means top performers have an incredibly high ROI because they produce over four times more than average workers.

When we pay disproportionate attention to our stars over our strugglers, at best we underutilise our stars, and at worst, we actively drive them away.

WE'RE NOT ADDRESSING UNDERPERFORMANCE QUICKLY ENOUGH

Positive workplace cultures can be double-edged swords. People who *love* where they work often do so because they love the *people* they work with. They have fun together. They respect each other. They consider each other friends, which is great on so many levels – and not so great when we need to address underperformance.

The Australian Government Fair Work Ombudsman classifies underperformance as one of four things:

1. Unsatisfactory work performance (failure to perform duties to the standard required).

2. Non-compliance with workplace policies, rules or procedures.

3. Unacceptable behaviour in the workplace.

4. Disruptive or negative behaviour that impacts co-workers.

Georgia Murch aptly calls this … *being a dick!* (Classic!)

Too often we let small things slide, because, well, they're small things. Mild lateness; corridor back-chat; rolling eyes. But these small things build up fast, and pretty soon we are flattened by the proverbial snowball.

Not addressing underperformance quickly enough is like letting someone with muddy shoes walk all over your pristine carpet. It's unsightly, difficult to clean, and often leaves a stain. If we wouldn't let someone muddy our carpet, why on Earth would we let disrespectful behaviour muddy our workplace environment?

Sometimes we forgive unacceptable or disruptive behaviour because we see people as rainmakers – people with special or hard-to-find skills who generate significant sales or save significant costs. We think we can't do without them. But a 2015 Harvard Business School study by Michael Housman and Dylan Minor of more than 50,000 employees across 11 firms found that a superstar performer, one who models desired values and delivers consistent performance, brings in more than US$5300 in cost savings to a company. Avoiding a toxic hire, or letting one go quickly, delivers US$12,500 in cost savings. In other words, these so-called 'rainmakers' may make us more in revenue, but they cost us more too, cancelling out any reason for excusing poor behaviour.

Bek Chee, Global Head of Talent at Atlassian, the $47 billion Australian software powerhouse, calls these people 'brilliant jerks'. She describes them as 'people who are extremely bright and talented with respect to the way they execute their role but aren't necessarily concerned with the impact they have on others'.

Atlassian's performance review system has changed to now place equal weight across three areas: job skills, impact on other team members, and living the company values. Atlassian says the change will 'more fairly measure people on how they bring their whole self to work'.

The Honourable David Hurley – Australia's Governor-General – told us that 'the standard you walk past is the standard you accept'. He was referring to discrimination against women in the defence forces and was actively empowering the entire institution to make a stand for change.

Being a leader means not walking past. It means holding ourselves and others accountable to higher standards. It means stepping outside our comfort zones and empowering ourselves with the tools and language to nip underperformance in the bud.

WE INVEST TIME GENERATING GREAT STRATEGIC PLANS BUT FAIL AT IMPLEMENTATION

Too many of us fall into the trap of investing time generating great Strategic Plans, only to fail at implementation.

In a *Harvard Business Review* article 'Turning Great Strategy into Great Performance', Michael Mankins and Richard Steele report that companies typically realise only about 60% of their strategies' potential value because of defects and breakdowns in planning and execution.

In 2004 they surveyed senior executives from 197 companies worldwide. They discovered that the strategy-to-performance gap can be attributed to a combination of factors, including:

- inadequate resources
- poorly communicated strategy
- actions required to execute not clearly defined
- unclear accountability for execution
- organisational silos and culture blocking execution
- inadequate performance monitoring

- inadequate consequences or rewards for failure or success

- poor or uncommitted leadership.

Every single one of these blockers comes back to leadership. Leaders influence how well strategy is utilised as a force for driving high performance.

Failing to extract full value from your Strategic Plan is about as wasteful as planning and paying for your dream holiday and not actually taking it! The secret to success is not just making a plan – it's implementing it.

A good test for whether your strategy plane has landed is to ask your newest employee these questions:

- Do you know what our strategic priorities are this quarter?

- How do our strategic priorities align with our company purpose and vision?

- What are the performance measures important to this business?

- How does your role add value and how do you measure your own success each day?

- How does what you do influence the success of the teams working around you?

If you're met with blank stares ... you have your answer.

WE FORGET THAT LEADERSHIP IS LEARNED

Many leaders are promoted to their position because they are great technical specialists, and they're given a team in an effort to add more value. They realise quickly they are ill-equipped to manage complex people dynamics, but don't want to admit it because, well, it's shameful to be promoted into a leadership role and not look like you know what you're doing! This compounds over time and quickly you have a stack of executives who are pretending to lead.

The challenge is, so much of leadership is paradoxical. To get people to do what needs to be done – we need to ask, not tell. To be perceived as courageous and resilient, we need to be vulnerable, not comfortable. To deepen trust and respect in a relationship, we need to give honest, raw feedback, not praise.

In her bestselling book *Dare to Lead*, Brené Brown tells us that the foundational skill of leadership is the willingness and ability to 'rumble with vulnerability':

> *A rumble is a discussion, conversation, or meeting defined by a commitment to lean into vulnerability, to stay curious and generous, to stick with the messy middle of problem identification and solving, to take a break and circle back when necessary, to be fearless in owning our parts and, as psychologist Harriet Lerner teachers, to listen with the same passion with which we want to be heard.*

Sound scary? Of course it is! Leading is terrifying! Embrace it.

If you're a leader and not feeling a little fear each day, you're living in denial, which is far more dangerous, because chances are the people around you are feeling your fear for you.

If you haven't mastered the art of leadership, don't beat yourself up. Recognise where you are and commit to learning the skills that will elevate your impact.

***

In learning The Leadership System, leaders inspire people to lift their performance in the service of a meaningful purpose and enable them to adopt the habits, behaviours and processes that ultimately drive results.

I asked Brad Sewell about how the playing group felt when they did not achieve their much anticipated second premiership within the five years set as part of their Five-2-Fifty strategic goal. He said:

> *The inability to achieve that strategic goal initially had absolutely no bearing or impact on the playing group. We became so focused on*

what our role was, which was to perform and to win games. It was broken down at such a granular level, whereby those lofty ambitions took care of themselves provided everybody adhered to the values and the structures.

Those so-called lofty ambitions weren't too far off – the group achieved three premierships in the three years following Five-2-Fifty.

Having a clear purpose and setting ambitious goals is one component to building a high-performing team. Leaders who invest their time wisely – who systematically set standards, normalise feedback and coach strengths – are the ones who convert lofty ambitions into the tangible results.

Part II summary

- The Leadership System is a process for ensuring the business purpose becomes the language and the actions of the business and the people within it.

- Like enzymes that act as catalysts for chemical reactions, inspiring leaders transform potential by leveraging talent in the pursuit of shared purpose.

- The Leadership System is a perpetual process of building capacity in people and inspiring high performance.

- Leaders inspire high performance when they consistently and systematically:

  - **set standards:** measurable benchmarks for performance that reflect the purpose and values of the organisation

  - **normalise feedback:** creating a team culture where it is normal to recognise behaviours that drive results, making it clear to those around you how to meet standards of performance

  - **coach strengths:** adopting an ask versus tell approach to help others leverage their strengths in the achievement of performance goals and standards.

- When leaders continually set standards, normalise feedback and coach strengths, they enable their people to quickly move through cycles of growth and amplify performance in structured and supported ways.

- When setting standards, set goals that are measurable, positively worded and aspirational.

- When giving feedback, get the quality right, and the quantity right:

  - give positive or negative constructive feedback, not praise or criticism

  - give positive constructive feedback on average six times more than negative constructive feedback.

- Feedback is constructive when it highlights specific behaviours that have a positive or negative impact on performance. Use the AID Model to give constructive feedback: **a**ctions, **i**mpact, **d**esired outcomes.

- To create feedback flow, where the push to give feedback is as strong as the pull to receive it, ask for it and role model how to receive feedback with grace and humility.

- When coaching, use GROW to activate innate intelligence and help people solve their own challenges. GROW is an acronym for a four-stage coaching conversation: **g**oals, **r**eality, **o**ptions, **w**ay forward.

- Have performance conversations to objectively assess when people meet pre-set goals and standards.

- Have development conversations to identify development goals and actions that enable ongoing learning and development in the role.

- Have behaviour conversations to highlight behaviours that align to organisational values.

- Leaders unwittingly enable low or mediocre performance by:
  - not giving enough attention to their best people
  - not addressing underperformance quickly enough
  - investing time in generating great Strategic Plans, but failing at implementation
  - promoting people with strong technical skills into leadership positions, without leadership training.

Part III

The Culture System

'Clients do not come first. Employees come first.
If you take care of your employees,
they will take care of the clients.'

Richard Branson

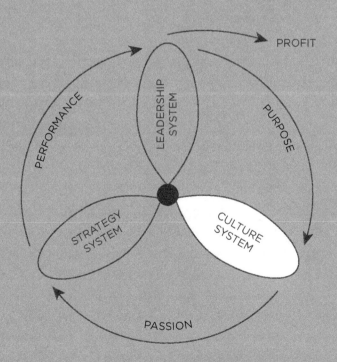

SWISSE WELLNESS

Swisse Wellness is an Australian success story. Founded in 1969 by Australian businessman and entrepreneur Kevin Ring who had the simple idea to improve people's lives with a range of naturally based, scientifically validated products, Swisse has been formulating premium health and wellness and beauty products for over 50 years.

The mission at Swisse Wellness is to make 'millions of people around the world Healthier and Happier (H+H)'. The vision is to be a Global Leading Wellness Brand and to CLED – that's Celebrate Life Every Day!

In September 2015, Swisse Wellness completed a landmark Australian transaction for A$1.67 billion with Hong Kong Stock Exchange–listed Biostime – one of the leading premium infant formula producers in Asia. This new partnership brought Swisse closer to its mission of becoming a global leading wellness brand by further positioning it strongly in the Chinese market.

Swisse Wellness attributes its success to three key factors. Their premium range of 200+ health, wellness and beauty products positioning them as a major player in the category. This coupled with significant investment in above-the-line marketing using high-profile ambassadors (think Nicole Kidman and Chris Hemsworth) has made them a household name. But by far and most importantly, they attribute their success to their people and entrepreneurial culture.

The Swisse Culture is grounded in the belief that if they focus on people, principles and passion, then profit will naturally follow. They call this their '4Ps' and they are the foundational values of the business, governing every decision from dealing with suppliers, to customers, to employees. Sound familiar? The Swisse 4Ps values were critical to driving success at Swisse, and had a big influence on my thinking about what leads to sustained high performance in organisations. So much so that one of the Swisse values – 'Passion' – has landed in my 3Ps model in this book.

To truly embed these values and communicate their commitment to people at a critical point in their growth just prior to a rapid expansion phase, Swisse Wellness created their Culture Plan in 2014.

The Culture Plan was a key one-page document that existed alongside the company one-page Business Plan. While the Business Plan mapped the company strategy for commercial growth; the Culture Plan ensured every team member was empowered to positively contribute in a healthy and happy way. The Culture Plan ensured that the vision, mission and values were upheld in achievement of business objectives.

The Culture Plan was created to articulate the many initiatives Swisse had in place to develop, support, engage and reward their team. All initiatives were clearly structured against their 4Ps – making the business accountable to living the values internally.

Measuring the effectiveness and impact of the Culture Plan was a key imperative in being accountable. Swisse utilised the scientifically validated tools from Human Synergistics; a company that specialises in the measurement and development of organisational culture and leadership. The Life-Styles Inventory (LSI) provided 360-degree feedback on the top 25 leaders of the business and insight into how their behaviour directly influenced team culture. The Organisational Culture Inventory (OCI) measured behavioural styles that mapped to the 4Ps values, known as Achievement, Self-Actualisation, Humanistic-Encouraging and Affiliative styles of behaviour. The Organisational Effectiveness Inventory (OEI) was used to measure outcomes of culture including engagement, team effectiveness and organisational effectiveness.

The Swisse CEO at the time, Radek Sali, led this change from the top. He participated in the program and was a strong advocate. He said in January 2016: 'With the aid of the LSI program, we are so proud of our achievements in enhancing our culture, giving our leaders the tools through feedback to become better leaders and in turn making our work place the best it can be.'

As a result of initiatives implemented from the Culture Plan, Swisse was recognised with several industry awards. Swisse Wellness was named as one of Great Place to Work's Top 25 in 2015 and 2016; the winner of the Australian Human Resources Institute (AHRI) Martin Seligman – Health and Wellbeing Award in 2015; and remained an Employer of Choice in the Australian Business Awards from 2016 to 2019. These awards cemented their employer brand in Australia and were an important attraction tool to the business.

The new owners fully embraced the company's unwavering commitment to the 4Ps core values; so much so, that on June 8, 2017, Biostime changed its name to the Health & Happiness (H+H) Group and adopted many of their cultural practices across their vast team in China.

The Swisse Wellness story demonstrates the critical factor of culture in driving high performance.

12

The power of culture

Culture drives engagement and ignites passion for your purpose. High-performance companies prioritise culture by putting their people first, and building their businesses around talent.

In his book *Good to Great*, Jim Collins positions leadership and culture before strategy. He defines 'great' companies as those that have delivered cumulative returns at least three times greater than the market over a 15-year period. Collins says companies that have gone from good to great all began their transformation by 'first getting the right people on the bus, the wrong people off the bus, and the right people in the right seats – and then they figured out where to drive it'. Collins believes that the old adage 'people are your most important asset' needs to be redefined. 'People are *not* your most important asset, the *right* people are,' he says.

Collins and his research team discovered that whether someone is the right person is less about their specific skills and capabilities and more about their character traits and innate capabilities. In other words – the right people are a good culture fit; they share your values and passion for the company's purpose.

CULTURE IS CRUCIAL

Human Synergistics, one of the world's leading companies measuring and consulting on cultural transformation, defines culture as:

The shared values, norms and expectations that govern the way people approach their work and interact with each other.

Human Synergistics measures culture against 12 different styles of thinking and behaviour, clustered as 'constructive', 'passive defensive' or 'aggressive defensive' styles.

In cultures that demonstrate predominantly constructive styles, people are encouraged to interact with each other in positive and supportive ways.

In these cultures, people balance a focus on task and goal achievement with a focus on people and relationships. They are described as 'humanistic' companies – companies that emphasise the learning, growth and wellbeing of their people in the achievement of business goals.

These cultures outperform cultures that demonstrate predominantly 'passive defensive' or 'aggressive defensive' styles of behaviour on a number of outcomes at the individual, team and organisational levels, delivering an average performance improvement across all three levels of 28%.

Compared to those working in predominantly 'passive defensive' or 'aggressive defensive' cultures, employees in 'constructive' cultures report:

- 26% more satisfaction

- 32% more motivation

- 19% greater role clarity

- 26% less stress

- 28% better teamwork

- 30% better inter-unit coordination

- 25% more commitment to departmental quality

- 32% greater perception of external adaptability

- 32% greater perception of organisational quality.

In a 2011 analysis of five Australian companies – Adshel, Mastercard, Yarra Valley Water, Richmond Football Club and Lion Nathan – Human Synergistics researchers also found improvements in revenue, EBIT, market share, engagement, staff retention and customer satisfaction as a direct result of culture transformation initiatives.

Gallup's most recent meta-analysis on team engagement and performance includes data on 1.8 million employees accumulated over the past two decades. Their analysis revealed that those in the top quartile of engagement outperformed those in the bottom quartile of engagement on a number of performance outcomes, including:

- 41% lower absenteeism

- 24% less turnover (in high-turnover organisations)

- 59% less turnover (in low-turnover organisations)

- 28% less shrinkage

- 70% fewer safety incidents

- 40% fewer quality defects

- 10% higher customer ratings

- 17% higher productivity

- 20% higher sales

- 21% higher profitability.

What does all this research tell us? It demonstrates that people's behaviour matters. You may have the world's greatest product and go-to-market strategy, but if you do not have a culture that emphasises constructive behaviour and healthy functioning of the human system, you will not have engaged employees and your business will never achieve high performance.

THE CULTURE LADDER

The culture ladder describes types of culture ranging from toxic (most defensive) to adaptive (most constructive) and what happens to the focus, behaviour and engagement levels of people under these conditions.

More constructive workplace cultures foster the conditions that drive workplace engagement, positively impacting business results. Conversely, more defensive cultures foster the conditions that drive disengagement, negatively impacting the bottom line.

The culture ladder

Culture	Focus on	Behaviour	Engaged-to-disengaged ratio
Adaptive	Learning	Innovative	90:10
Inclusive	Belonging	Collaborative	75:25
Siloed	Fitting in	Conforming	50:50
Defensive	Protection	Avoidant	25:75
Toxic	Attack	Hostile	10:90

Let's have a look at each of these, starting from the bottom up.

Toxic cultures

In **toxic** cultures, people focus on **attack** and behave in **hostile** ways. Hostile behaviours manifest as resistance to new ideas, abruptness, controlling or dominating the air time, recklessness, exclusion, discrimination, blaming others for mistakes or outright criticism. People in toxic cultures adopt these defence mechanisms in order to maintain their own status in what are highly competitive workplace environments. Competition can be a great motivator when it is focused externally on the marketplace. But it is destructive to cultures when focused internally, leading to fights for positional power, status or authority. It is difficult to establish trust in these environments, because people constantly question one another's motives. In these environments, the majority of the workforce is **disengaged** or even **actively disengaged** – they actively talk about their disappointment and disillusionment both inside and outside the organisation, and are more or less out to damage either their colleagues' reputation or the whole company's reputation. Gallup research reveals that 73% of actively disengaged employees are actively looking for a new job (compared to 37% of engaged employees).

Defensive cultures

In **defensive** cultures, people focus on **protection** and behave in **avoidant** ways. They focus their energies on defending their own territories, not getting involved in tasks or priorities that sit outside their own teams or extending themselves beyond the responsibilities that sit strictly inside their own role boundaries. People avoid responsibility and accountability for fear of being wrongly criticised or blamed when things don't go to plan. In these environments, a large proportion of the workforce remains **disengaged** – they show up and go through the motions, doing the bare minimum to get by. They've essentially 'checked out'.

In toxic or defensive cultures, there is no psychological safety – the interpersonal risk associated with 'sticking your neck out' is too great. The fear of being publicly humiliated and risking your reputation in these cultures is not just imagined – it's real and tangible. When people spend vast amounts of psychological energy protecting themselves from real or imagined threats, they have little left to extend themselves creatively or otherwise. This wastes human potential and undermines the capacity of the organisation to achieve its purpose.

Siloed cultures

In **siloed** cultures, people focus on **fitting in** and behave in **conform-ing** ways. They focus their energies on fitting in with their own teams and areas of the business in order to gain the approval and acceptance of their work group. While these environments seem pleasant on the surface, they hide a great deal of underlying tension because conflicts are not dealt with openly – either within or between teams. Individuals in these organisations conform to their silos, making it more difficult to achieve alignment on shared objectives. This results in a **neutral** or ambivalent workforce; 50% are engaged, 50% are disengaged.

Inclusive cultures

In **inclusive** cultures, people focus on **belonging** and behave in **collaborative** ways. **Belonging** is seen as more important than fitting in – people are encouraged to bring their full selves to work; diversity is valued and able to be worked with. Individuals work in teams but easily work across the business both horizontally and vertically in the service of shared objectives. A majority of the workforce in these organisations are **engaged** – they are enthusiastic about, involved in, and committed to their work and willingly give their discretionary effort – going above and beyond the minimum required to get the job done.

Adaptive cultures

In **adaptive** cultures, people focus on **learning** and behave in **innovative** ways. They focus their energies on **learning** in the service of growth for people, teams and the organisation as a whole. In these environments, people are **engaged** or even **actively engaged** – they are openly enthusiastic about their employee experience. Cultures like these sustain and perpetuate high performance.

***

How would you describe your culture? What impact is that having on where you focus your energy, how you behave and your level of engagement?

If you feel that the culture of your team or workplace is anything less than adaptive, The Culture System is a proven process that will evolve your culture towards a more constructive and engaging experience.

13

Introducing
The Culture System

The Culture System involves the creation and communication of:

- your purpose beyond profit – how you add value to all stakeholders of your business

- your values and behaviours – how you *behave* in the pursuit of your purpose or company mission

- a Culture Plan that clearly communicates how you live your values at each stage of the employee lifecycle.

Implementing The Culture System will ensure that you live and honour your values and maintain the engagement and wellbeing of your people, resulting in increased capacity for high performance.

The Culture System

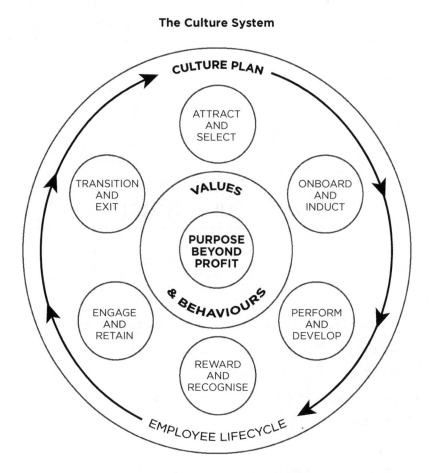

Let's have a look at each of these elements.

PURPOSE BEYOND PROFIT

Jim Collins's research drills down into companies that have gone from good to great and that are built to last. And then there are companies that people *love* – companies that generate value equally across all stakeholder groups, including suppliers, partners, investors, customers, employees and the environment. These are the companies with clear and memorable purpose statements that translate into tangible employee and customer experiences.

Companies with clear purpose describe not just *what* they do and *how* they do it, but *why* they exist. Purpose statements are memorable when they are short and sharp; specific and clear; aspirational and enduring.

VALUES AND BEHAVIOURS

Values sit at the core of an organisation and influence how people behave in the pursuit of the company's purpose. Values can't be seen – but they can be observed by how people behave when working together, serving customers, and making decisions about what to prioritise and act on.

Being clear on your company values is an important attraction and retention tool. Get the right people 'on the bus' by finding those with similar values and beliefs – those who share your passions and commitments for generating value in your chosen market.

To truly make values tangible and measurable, it's also important to describe the behaviours that align with the company values – what does it look like when you are living your values, and when you are not?

THE CULTURE PLAN

For values to have any meaning and support in a business, they must be authentic.

The Culture Plan is the company's commitment to living their values through every touchpoint in the employee lifecycle. The Culture Plan is a simple plan on a page that clearly outlines the company purpose, values, and key benefits that deliver an exceptional employee experience.

Delivering on the Culture Plan is a shared responsibility between leaders, employees and the People & Culture team (who may be either in house or externally based). The Culture Plan is as important as the Business Plan in driving high performance.

HOW THE CULTURE SYSTEM FUELS PASSION

After leaving Swisse Wellness as CEO, Radek Sali went on to found Light Warrior investments. At the time of writing, he is Light Warrior's Chairperson and sits on multiple boards spanning both private and non-profit sectors. As part of the research for this book, I interviewed Radek to ask for his reflections on what drives high-performance:

> *The best thing you can do is make sure you have an extraordinary culture ... The culture itself demands everyone in that organisation bring their best self and to not take the easy road but be rewarded for bringing their best to work.*

Culture fuels passion by connecting people to a shared system of values and beliefs. Progressive CEOs like Radek understand that culture and strategy are equally important in driving performance outcomes, and that these things are delivered by leadership. The CEO and leadership team play a critical role in supporting culture and change initiatives:

> *For me, if you don't have a Culture Plan and a Business Plan, you won't be successful. When I ask, generally people say they've got a Business Plan. And that's great, but what you need is that overlay of culture – how you're going to go about doing it, and your reason for doing it. The Culture Plan brings the Business Plan to life and makes it relevant, so we feel really engaged and purposeful when we do our work.*

In high-performance cultures, everybody lifts to bring their best game. People are encouraged to challenge each other and speak up, no matter their status or authority in the business. No single individual is above the culture, not even the founder or the CEO. These cultures create legacies; operating rhythms that pull people in and generate enormous amounts of energy and passion from everyone who works within them.

14

Purpose beyond profit

Your purpose is your primary reason for being. It is the difference you make, the value you add, the change you create.

The terms 'purpose' and 'mission' have been used interchangeably. More recently we've seen 'purpose' claiming its moment alone in the spotlight, with its more nuanced definition encompassing value beyond profit or investor returns.

Purpose can also be likened to the notion of an organisation's 'primary spirit'. (I love this idea that an organisation can have a spirit.) Alistair and Joshua Bain introduced the notion of primary spirit in an article published in *Socio-Analysis* as an adjunct to Albert Kenneth Rice's concept of 'primary task' – or 'that which the organisation must do to survive'. If the primary task is *what* the organisation does, the primary spirit is *why* the organisation exists. Bain & Bain defined primary spirit as 'that which gives meaning to the primary task'; or 'that which breathes life into an organisation: the animating principle'.

┃ **Purpose-driven organisations take a balanced view of success.**

They measure their worth in terms of value-add across multiple stakeholder groups, including investors, customers, employees, suppliers, community and the environment.

A growing number of business leaders globally are taking more responsibility, asking themselves how they can be accountable not just for delivering a healthy bottom line, but for the social, environmental and economic dilemmas that plague us all.

These business leaders understand that governments, non-profits and social service organisations can't tackle these problems alone. They realise that capitalism can, in fact, be harnessed as a force for good.

TRULY COMMITTING TO PURPOSE

The growing movement of purpose beyond profit is finding its voice through organisations like B Corp, The B Team, Conscious Capitalism, and 1% for the Planet.

The Business Roundtable, an association of CEOs of leading US companies, issued a statement on organisational purpose in 2019. It contends that companies should no longer focus on advancing the interests of shareholders alone – they must also deliver value to customers, invest in their employees, protect the environment, support the communities in which they work, and deal fairly with suppliers. These CEOs agree that, 'Each of our stakeholders is essential. We commit to deliver value to all of them, for the future success of our companies, our communities and our country'.

The statement is signed by almost 200 CEOs, and serves as a template for all businesses seeking to expand their corporate social responsibility agenda.

FIRMS OF ENDEARMENT

Being a purpose-driven organisation pays off in ways that outstrip not just S&P500 companies but also the 'great' companies reported in Jim Collins's research.

Raj Sisodia is the co-founder and Chairman of Conscious Capitalism and co-author of *Firms of Endearment* alongside Jag Sheth and David Wolfe. In their book, the authors describe 'firms of endearment' (FoEs) as the ultimate humanistic companies – seeking to maximise value in ways that stakeholders respect, admire and even love. FoEs *endear* themselves to stakeholders by bringing the interests of all stakeholder groups into strategic alignment, without favouring one over the other.

The authors identified FoEs by searching out companies that exemplified high standards of humanistic performance. Put simply, they looked for companies that were loved – and importantly, were loved by *all* stakeholder groups. Then they conducted an investor analysis to understand the financial performance of these companies. This is how their research approach differed from Jim Collins's work – who started first with an investor analysis and then an internal analysis of drivers of performance.

Raj and his colleagues expected that the firms they researched would demonstrate performance equal to or perhaps marginally stronger than the industry average. They did not anticipate what they found. Not only did FoEs outperform the S&P500 by *14 times*, they also outstripped Jim Collins's 'great' companies by *six times* over a period of 15 years. Their research is reported on their website and in the new edition of their book.

So, what defines a Firm of Endearment? FoEs are differentiated by a number of attributes. They typically demonstrate:

- active alignment of all stakeholder groups
- relatively modest executive salaries
- open-door policies at every level, including the executive level

- employee benefits and compensation greater than the industry standard

- considerably more time devoted to employee training

- lower turnover than industry average

- employees empowered to make customers happy (without needing to seek management approval)

- conscious effort to hire people who are passionate about the company and its products

- a genuine passion for customers

- lower marketing costs (because their customers and employees become their biggest advocates)

- genuine efforts to help suppliers reach higher productivity, quality and profitability – resulting in suppliers who line up to work with them

- consideration of corporate culture as a genuine asset

- innovative and fast adaption to market trends and opportunities.

All of this adds up to a company where people are passionate. Passionate about the product, passionate about the customer experience, and passionate about the brand. The collective energy for these companies lifts engagement and minimises costs. People who work in these companies go to extraordinary lengths to innovate, adapt, and serve – because they feel valued, appreciated, and part of a worthy and meaningful purpose.

People stay because they are trusted, challenged, and experience professional growth, minimising turnover and recruitment costs and keeping the intellectual property (IP) in the business. People line up to join them – giving these companies the selection of the best talent and freeing up management to focus on strategy execution instead of replenishing the team. Customers talk about them – on social media, to their friends – which reduces the need for marketing spend. Suppliers and partners work collaboratively with them – because it's a mutually beneficial relationship and they will do what is necessary to maintain it. These companies create win–win situations, and ultimately this passion for the business, if harnessed with clear strategy, translates into profit.

NOW THAT'S SPICE-E

Sisodia, Sheth & Wolfe identify five major stakeholder groups whom FoEs consider equally important and whose shared interests they strive to meet:

- society
- partners
- investors
- customers
- employees.

(SPICE for short.)

In addition to these groups, I propose we all must consider an additional stakeholder – the environment. In chapter 3, Stone & Wood were examined as one such company who considers their impact on the environment and creates business strategies that support and sustain positive environmental outcomes. Businesses play a key role in mitigating climate change by minimising waste, reducing their footprint and investing in new energy-efficient technologies. We all must consider the planet as our ultimate stakeholder and make a commitment to sustainable business practices.

The addition of environment to the SPICE model makes it SPICE-E!

MAKE YOUR PURPOSE STATEMENT MEMORABLE

To truly ignite passion, your purpose statement must reflect that your business serves a genuine purpose beyond profit.

> Purpose statements, when expressed simply and uniquely, are powerful tools that build passion and energy for your brand because they are memorable and repeatable.

Good purpose statements are:

- **Short and sharp**, preferably no more than 10 words. They need to be statements that your team can remember and repeat; like an organisational mantra. Descriptive statements have a place as the subtext to your purpose statement. But if you can't summarise your purpose in a single repeatable statement, you're not being succinct enough. A basic rule: if you can remember it, you've nailed it!

- **Specific and clear.** They should be authentic to you and clearly reflect your brand. Many mission statements are generalisations. They could sit on any company charter. Stacey Barr, author of *Prove It!*, talks about the importance of avoiding clichéd or pedestrian mission statements: 'When our vision, our purpose, our direction are specific and clear, they are compelling.'

- **Aspirational and enduring.** They are always aspirational in nature, giving your company something to reach for that is a permanent and enduring. Strategic goals and priorities change as companies grow and evolve; but your purpose, your reason for being, never changes.

Here are some great examples of purpose statements that meet this brief:

- 'Spread ideas' – TED

- 'We deliver' – Australia Post

- 'To inspire and develop the builders of tomorrow' – Lego

- 'To create happiness for all people of all ages, everywhere' – Disney

- 'To bring transportation – for everyone, everywhere' – Uber
- 'To accelerate the world's transition to sustainable energy' – Tesla
- 'Making millions around the world healthier and happier' – Swisse Wellness
- 'Beer as a force for good' – Stone and Wood Brewing Company
- 'To be Earth's most customer-centric company' – Amazon
- 'We're in business to save our home planet' – Patagonia
- 'We save people money so they can live better' – Walmart
- 'To help bring creative projects to life' – Kickstarter
- 'To help people around the world plan and have the perfect trip' – TripAdvisor
- 'Bring inspiration and innovation to every athlete in the world' – Nike
- 'To build the Web's most convenient, secure, cost-effective payment solution' – Paypal
- 'To make it easy to do business anywhere' – Alibaba Group
- 'Making travel dreams come true' – TripADeal
- 'To connect the world's professionals to make them more productive and successful' – LinkedIn

By contrast, here are examples that are aspirational and specific, yet not short and sharp (and therefore difficult to remember or repeat):

- 'To be Earth's most customer-centric company, where customers can find and discover anything they might want to buy online, and endeavors to offer its customers the lowest possible prices.' – Amazon
- 'To deliver information on the people, ideas and technologies changing the world to our community of affluent business decision makers.' – Forbes

- 'To enable economic growth through infrastructure and energy development, and to provide solutions that support communities and protect the planet.' – CAT

Finally, here are some examples that are short and sharp, aspirational and enduring, yet not specific and clear enough (they could appear on any company website):

- 'To be a company that inspires and fulfils your curiosity' – Sony

- 'To enable people and businesses throughout the world to realize their full potential' – Microsoft

- 'Improving people's lives through meaningful innovation' – Philips

- 'To improve every life through innovative giving in education, community and the environment' – 3M

- 'Living and breathing diversity and inclusion in how we work every day' – Canva.

All these purpose statements are perfectly good statements. My goal here is not to criticise companies – but to make an example of the kind of statement that will take root in people's minds and direct both thinking and decision making on a daily basis.

If you're going to build a purpose statement, build one that makes you stand out from the crowd and is memorable enough to be talked about.

INCLUDE YOUR WHY, HOW AND WHAT

Simon Sinek's three little words – *why, how, what* – is a simple and effective tool for capturing your company's purpose statement. Sinek says:

- Every organisation knows **what** they do. These are products they sell or services they offer.

- Some organisations know **how** they do it. These are the things that make them special or set them apart from the competition; their USP (unique selling proposition), proprietary process or differentiating value proposition.

- Very few organisations know **why** they do what they do. *Why* is not about making money; that's the result. Your *why* is the reason you exist.

Sinek says that great leaders and great companies start with why – they talk about themselves from the 'inside out' or from why, to how, to what. This is because 'people don't buy what you do, they buy why you do it'. When it comes to a purchasing decision between two products of similar price and quality, the deciding factor comes down to what your brand stands for and whether the buyer's personal values align with your brand's perceived values. In fact, Sinek's research shows that buyers will pay more for brands they feel aligned with.

By answering all three questions, you make it easy for your customers and employees to know:

- why you exist – how you add value to their lives

- how you are unique – how you do business differently and why they should buy from you versus your competitors

- what you do – the tangible products and services that deliver on your purpose.

Not only does this make their purchasing decisions much easier, but it builds an army of people who advocate for your brand on your behalf.

HOW TO CRAFT YOUR PURPOSE STATEMENT

To build a purpose statement, the first step is to go to your people. You need to involve the key representatives of your organisation, which necessarily includes the founders, senior people, longest serving employees and customer-facing staff. But, ideally, it includes the whole organisation. Workshops are a great way to systematically work through the why, how and what questions. Here's how you could set it up:

1. To answer the *why* question, ask everyone to form small groups to discuss and capture notes to these questions:

   - Why would you choose [insert company name] over any other company?
   - When you purchase/experience [insert company name] products or services, what are your expectations?
   - What do you want to walk away feeling from a [insert company name] experience?

2. Based on your answers to the questions above, discuss as a group your responses to this sentence: [Insert company name] exists to:

   - A
   - B
   - C

3. Collate and distil everyone's responses to question 2 into a single statement that captures the essence of them all.

4. Test the statement – is it short and sharp? Is it simple and clear? Is it aspirational and enduring? Keep working at it until it meets all three criteria.

5. To answer the *how* and *what* questions, ask everyone in small groups to discuss and capture a one-sentence answer to these questions:

   - How are our processes or ways of working unique and special? How are we different to our competitors?
   - What are we? What do we actually do for our customers?

6. Collate and distil everyone's sentences into single *how* and *what* statements that capture the essence of them all.

The content produced from your workshops will inform both the purpose statement and the descriptive statements that may exist alongside them and appear on your website and internal culture assets. It's essential that the purpose statement resonates, is memorable and truly describes why you exist.

15

Defining company values and behaviours

If your purpose describes *why* you exist, *how* you are unique, and *what* you do, your values capture how you *behave* in the pursuit of your company mission.

> **Values provide an essential moral compass to your business.**

They define what is important; what is of 'value' or considered valuable. Here's the trick though. Values can't be seen. We learn from each other what our values are by observing and experiencing the behaviours, attitudes, responses and practices that naturally arise during our interactions with people.

The behaviours you see are the indicators of the values held within. Therefore, for people to be meaningfully held accountable to a set of values or ethical standards, the behaviours that exemplify your values must be defined.

WHAT ARE VALUES?

The iceberg model is an oldie but a goodie for explaining how values are expressed. This model can be traced back to Edward T. Hall (an American anthropologist who was born in 1914) and is often called upon to explain how values work. Just like the tip of an iceberg, what is seen above the surface of the water is only a small proportion of what lies below it. People's behaviours are the tip of the iceberg. What drives behaviour, the largest proportion of who we are, sits beneath the surface of the water – our thoughts and feelings, values and beliefs, and driving needs.

People's behaviours are the tip of the iceberg

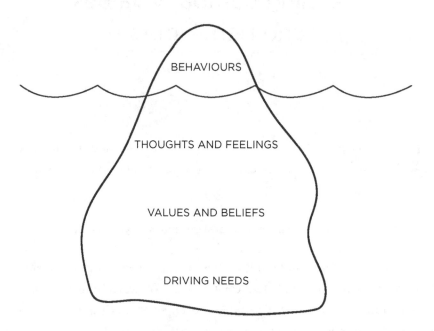

Let's have a look at each of these elements.

Behaviours

Behaviours are our actions and words. They are what we can see. Often we make assumptions about people's intentions based on what we see. But you can't know what's really behind someone's actions unless you ask what they think and feel, what is important to them, what their needs are. You can only know what is driving behaviour by going under the surface of the water.

Thoughts and feelings

These sit just below the surface of the water. They are accessible to us in our conscious mind. If I ask you what you are currently thinking and feeling, you'll be able to answer easily.

Values and beliefs

Values and beliefs sit a bit deeper. They influence how we think and feel, but they are not as readily accessible. If I ask what your values and beliefs are, unless you've given it a lot of thought or done some personal development work, you might not be able to answer that question straight away. You'll probably need to go away and think about it.

Our values and beliefs are formed early in life. They are instilled in us by observing the actions and words of our parents and caregivers within the context of our cultural community. Once they're set by about the age of seven, they're with us for life. In this way, values are transmitted through generations and are part of our cultural programming.

Driving needs

Driving needs sit at the deepest level of our psyche. Abraham Maslow defined our needs as a pyramid, with physiological needs at the base (air, water, food, shelter, sleep, sex), followed by our needs for safety (security, employment, health, wealth), love and belonging (family, friendship, intimacy, community), esteem (respect, status, recognition, freedom) and self-actualisation (realisation of potential) at the very pinnacle. These are universally experienced core human drivers, and they build upon each other – we cannot experience self-actualisation without first satisfying all other needs. We are very rarely conscious of our needs, and accessing them requires deep intuitive reflection.

NEEDS VERSUS VALUES

While needs are *universal* and necessary to the survival of the human race, values are *cultural* and necessary to the survival of a particular psycho-social group. Values drive behaviours that ensure survival and flourishing within a specific geographic region; socio-demographic, political or religious context; or free-trade market. By defining and reinforcing company values we set standards for behaviour that drive success for our own specific organisation or operating context. Values are markers for people, calling those who share similar values, who will be most likely to be successful or flourish in your specific operating context. Values indicate what we deem as positive, what we recognise and what we reward.

WHO'S ON *YOUR* BUS?

When making important decisions about who to hire and who to keep on the bus, I like using an analogy shared by Jim Collins about asking yourself this question ... if you were at the bottom of Mt Everest; who would you place your absolute trust and faith in to join you on that journey to the top? Of course – physical fitness would be a given. But say you had a group from whom to select who all passed the physical tests – what would you base your decisions on then?

You'd choose those most resilient; those who put the needs of others ahead of their own; those who are strategic, organised and planned; those who are patient, kind and resourceful; those who are able to manage themselves; and those who talk about your mission with the same level of passion and drive as you do. You'd choose people who demonstrate, through their behaviour, your values for persistence, endurance, courage, achievement, empathy and above all leadership.

In his book *Traction*, Gino Wickman uses a simple tool he calls the 'people analyser' to assess whether you have the right people on the bus. He suggests listing your people's names in a column down the left, and your core values in the row across the top. Then rate each person according to his or her demonstration of those values. Give them one of three ratings:

+   She or he exhibits that core value most of the time

+/–   She or he exhibits that core value sometimes

–   She or he doesn't exhibit that core value most of the time

This is just one tool you can use to support the most important decisions you need to make as an employer or leader. A tool such as this could be used as part of formal reviews or when having behaviour conversations (outlined in chapter 6). By hiring and keeping people who share the same core values, you maintain a solid base from which to climb the mountain – whatever that mountain represents in your context.

BUILDING VALUES AND BEHAVIOURS

A set of clearly defined values is the lynchpin of your culture.

To successfully define and live your values, they need to achieve two things:

1. They need to satisfy the same criteria as a purpose statement. That is, they need to be **short and sharp**; **specific and clear**; **aspirational and enduring**.

2. They need to define the behaviours that align with the values. What does it look like when we are living our values? What is it *not*?

MAKE VALUES STATEMENTS MEMORABLE

Compare these four sets of values statements:

Company 1
Excellence
Innovation
Customer fixation
Teamwork
Community
Fun

Company 2

Focus on the user and all else will follow.

It's best to do one thing really, really well.

Fast is better than slow.

Democracy on the web works.

You don't need to be at your desk to need an answer.

You can make money without doing evil.

There's always more information out there.

The need for information crosses all borders.

You can be serious without a suit.

Great just isn't good enough.

Company 3

Open company, no bullshit

Build with heart and balance

Don't #@!% the customer

Play as a team

Be the change you seek

Company 4

Reach

Learn

Di-bear-sity

Colla-bear-ate

Give

Cele-bear-ate

Which set of values are you more endeared to? Which set are you more likely to remember?

While these are all great examples of company values, they are not the same in terms of memorability and impact.

Company 1's values are those of Yahoo. Great company – very successful. But these values could sit on any company values charter. They do not speak of the unique personality of that company and are therefore less memorable.

Company 2's values belong to Yahoo's main competitor, Google. They certainly speak authentically to that company's unique personality and culture, but there are too many to easily remember and recite. It would take time in the company and multiple repetitions to remember those values and easily share them with incoming employees.

Company 3's values belong to Atlassian, Australia's fastest growing software company. These are getting much better – they are short and sharp, unique and memorable. No other company has these values. They speak directly to Atlassian's target employee – someone who values radical honesty, accountability, and a strong customer focus.

Company 4's values are by far the most creative and most endearing set of values I've come across so far. They belong to Build-A-Bear, a global company based in the US who specialise in stores where children can build their own teddy bears. How can you not want to know more about that brand when you see company values like that? In addition to being short, sharp, and memorable, they've invented new words that are totally unique to their company and position them as a fun, caring and inspiring place to work or take your children.

Make values usable by defining behaviours

Having a set of unique and memorable values is only half of the equation. Sadly – too many companies miss out on the opportunity to uphold values by failing to define what it looks like when we are living them. By not defining behaviours, we leave too much up to subjectivity. One person's version of what 'Colla-bear-ation' looks like is going to be different to the next. To make your values meaningful and usable, you must describe the *behaviours* that align with those values. What does it look like when we are living that value? And what is it not?

Only when you describe a set of behaviours that align with values do you make values observable and measurable. You then empower leaders to have behaviour conversations; to give feedback in order to reinforce positive behaviours that align with values; and discourage negative behaviours that undermine values.

Moose Toys is an Australian-owned company and one of the world's largest toy manufacturers. They pride themselves on building a company culture based on fun, playfulness, and creativity. They know their success relies on happy, innovative people coming up with ingenious ways to delight and excite children. Their company website and social media espouse a company that puts values at the heart of their business: 'Our values are the essence of our identity – our DNA – "The Moose Way". They are our guiding principles that underpin everything we do – both internally and externally'. Moose Toys have three core company values, stated as a sentence:

We're a Family, who is Outrageously Playful, with a Wild Imagination.

What does **Outrageously Playful** look like at Moose Toys? No … it's not about playing table tennis all day or pulling pranks on each other. For Moosies (as they call their people), Outrageously Playful looks like:

- *Playing to stimulate thinking and innovation – applying learning across all initiatives.*

- *Thinking outside the toy box to keep things super fun.*

- *Consistently giving 100% to put the punch in our products and services.*

- *Keeping our energy up so there's a great buzz around the place all the time – helping to foster great ideas and ensuring strong productivity.*

Those behaviours make it crystal clear what living the value of Outrageously Playful is at Moose Toys, so it's easy for people to give feedback to each other on whether those values are being lived.

Swisse Wellness take their behaviour statements to another level. As well as defining what it looks like to demonstrate those values, they define what it's *not*.

For example, let's see how they define their 'people' value:

Value	What it is	What it's not
PEOPLE **People always come first**	Putting people first is: Treating each other with respect, fairness and empathy. Celebrating diversity, valuing each others' contribution, showing support, and being genuinely happy for each others' success. Creating, seeking and relishing opportunities to Learn, Grow and Improve.	Putting people first is not: Working in silos – the greatest results come from team efforts. Talking behind each others' backs, gossiping and deriding individuals or the company. Blaming others – being unaccountable and not taking ownership.

Your behaviours statements are not comprehensive lists that become unwieldy and impossible to manage. They are the three key behaviours you absolutely want to see more of, and the three key behaviours you absolutely will not accept or tolerate. You must be selective with them.

By doing this work, you make the implicit, explicit. You empower people with the tools to assess at performance review times and in behaviour conversations.

A basic structure to build out your values and behaviours code is by using the following table for each value.

Value	What it is	What it's not
Short descriptive statement	Behaviour 1. Behaviour 2. Behaviour 3.	Behaviour 1. Behaviour 2. Behaviour 3.

How to define your values and behaviours

The thing is, values aren't something you decide. Values are something you *discover*.

They are already present when groups of people come together. We discover them by observing the ways in which those people interact when they are delivering a product or service to internal or external stakeholders.

What we are trying to do when we define a set of company values is identify the positive core of the organisation. What exists that connects, aligns and inspires us? What shared beliefs bind us together and ultimately drive our thoughts, feelings and behaviours?

There are a number of useful methods to discover the values and beliefs that exist within groups, and the appreciative inquiry (AI) method devised by Dr David Cooperrider is one of them.

AI is a scientifically proven strengths-based change approach. It is a process by which we explore what is working in organisations and amplify those strengths, rather than focusing on fixing problems or weaknesses. The approach is based on the premise that human systems move in the direction of the questions they ask. If organisations focus on problems and issues, they often unconsciously magnify the very issues they are trying to solve.

AI is a four-stage process called the 4D framework. The stages are:

- **Discover:** What gives life? What is our positive core?

- **Dream:** What do we look like at our best?

- **Design:** What are the pathways to turn our dreaming into reality?

- **Destiny:** What are our commitments to action? What are our next steps?

The 'discover' stage of the 4D framework reveals the core values that exist at the heart of any group. This activity can be run with your whole organisation split into smaller groups or teams (depending on your size), or with a select group of people who are a representative sample of the wider system. The key here is to involve a broad range of people, not just 'special groups' such as senior people or those with the longest tenure. You may even ask your people to nominate a committee whom they believe are exemplars of your company culture. This process facilitates greater buy in, because there is already a high level of trust in the people whose output you know the rest of the team will trust and respect.

THE 'VALUES DISCOVERY' SESSION

1. Gather your people or selected representatives in a 'values discovery' session.

2. In pairs, ask people to interview each other using the following set of questions:
   - What first attracted you to our company?
   - What makes you proud to work in our company?
   - What is unique about the way we treat each other in our company?
   - Think back to two examples that you've seen or heard that describes us at our **best**.

3. Ask each pair to join up with another pair and share each other's stories from the interviews, capturing on a piece of flipchart paper (pictured below) the key stories down the left side; and then the root causes of success (the underlying values driving success) down the right side.

4. Once the root causes of success are listed, ask each group to agree on one word that captures the essence of each root cause of success. These are the values that are driving success.

5. Collate all the values, cluster them into themes, and agree on the top three to five values.

6. Express those values in your own language; and seek a list of three specific behaviours from the 'stories of success' that best exemplify those values.

Stories	Root causes of success
Lived experiences of your organisation at its best	Underlying values driving success

REINFORCING VALUES

Values are truly put to the test when employers are faced with a decision to keep or let go of their 'brilliant jerks'. These are the people we met in chapter 11: they are very talented at what they do, but don't support others around them or demonstrate the company's values.

> **What do you do when you're faced with a decision to let go of rainmakers who also happen to be jerks?**

You follow through. Take the short-term hit to play the long-term game.

Not delivering on your promise to hold people accountable for repeated behavioural offenses is a surefire way to render your company values meaningless, kill engagement in your business and generate disenchantment for your employer brand. No-one, no matter how effective their results, is above the company culture. Holding onto your 'brilliant jerks' is a short-term 'solution' that will eventually erode performance and engagement across the whole group.

As you will read in the next chapter on the Culture Plan, company values, once defined, are reinforced by threading them through every touchpoint in the employee lifecycle.

Reinforcing values is achieved through a number of mechanisms:

- **Values questions in recruitment:** asking questions that uncover where new candidates' values align with the company values.

- **Values induction sessions:** inducting new starters into your values – what they are, the behaviours that align, how the values were formed, who the founders are and why these values are important to them, and stories of where the company lived them.

- **Values as a KPI:** incorporating behaviours conversations as part of formal reviews.

- **Values rewards:** Celebrating and calling out those who demonstrate values – making them your company heroes.

- **Values on every job description and employment contract –** making it clear that performance incorporates both task accomplishment and behaviour.

- **Values talked about in every CEO address –** values are revisited in every CEO presentation, and used in her or his everyday language.

These and several other mechanisms are discussed in the following chapter.

16

The Culture Plan

The Culture Plan is an organisational asset that demonstrates, at a glance, how your company honours its values in the ways it deals with employees at each stage of the employee lifecycle.

If you expect high performance from every person in the business, which includes upholding the espoused values and behaviours, then it is only fair that this be reciprocated, and the business uphold the values in how it deals with people.

The Culture Plan operationalises your Culture System (your espoused purpose, values and behaviours), enabling leaders to honour values with the subsequent structures, processes and incentives that drive high performance.

For values to have any meaning in a business, they must be authentic. If you have a set of corporate values that are incongruent with what people observe and experience through their interactions with each other, then your values statements are empty and can actually become a demotivator – a constant reminder of how the organisation fails to stack up to expectations. Conversely, when your espoused values *are* congruent with your employees' experiences, this becomes a key engagement and motivator to high performance.

THE EMPLOYEE LIFECYCLE

For values to be lived and to truly influence culture they must be demonstrated at every touchpoint of your employees' experience. Much like mapping your customer experience, the employee lifecycle is framework that helps you map the employee experience.

Let's take a look at some of the typical stages of the employee lifecycle, and how you might demonstrate your values at each step.

The employee lifecycle

Attract and select

The attract and select stage is the first point of contact that employees have with your brand. It's the point at which they decide whether your company is the right fit for them. The employee experience at this stage is influenced by the brand image you project online, as well as the nature of your interview and recruitment process.

The **attraction and selection** experience can be enhanced by:

- including a clear *About Us* section on your website, sharing the company purpose, values and vision, and providing information about the board, founders and senior executives who may be easily searched and reviewed on social media

- encouraging employees who are listed on LinkedIn to include consistent descriptions of the company in their profiles

- encouraging executives who are listed on LinkedIn to talk about, share and comment on posts that are congruent with your company values and ethics

- creating well-designed job descriptions that include: the company purpose and values; the job title and job summary; key accountabilities and KPIs; and desired skills and qualifications

- conducting recruitment interviews where candidates are assessed not just for their strengths fit but also for culture fit, with behavioural questions targeted at discovering core values alignment.

The nature of questions asked in an interview sends the first signals as to whether your company would be a great place to work. Assess for strengths – what people both love doing and are naturally good at. Understand their passions for the business and product or service, inquire about long-term career aspirations, and what professional development opportunities they are seeking. Finally, ask them about your company values – what resonates most strongly and why?

ACING THE JOB DESCRIPTION

Building the right level of detail into a job description is an art form all of its own. A good job description is both specific and succinct. As a general rule, to make job descriptions compelling and meaningful, they should be no longer than two pages – and only target the specific accountabilities and skills that are relevant to that job, avoiding generic statements that could appear on any job description (like 'organisational skills' and 'attention to detail' – name me one job that doesn't require these skills).

A good job description includes:

- the company purpose statement and company values clearly positioned at the top

- the job title

- reporting manager and direct reports (if any)

- a two- or three-sentence position summary that captures the essence of the role

- the key performance indicator(s) for the role – what is *the* key measurable of that role?

- roles and responsibilities – chunked up into three core responsibilities with perhaps two or three bullet points describing each one

- desired qualifications and experience.

Onboard and induct

You only get one chance to make a first impression. Onboarding and induction is a major opportunity to win hearts and gain enduring employee commitment. A poorly planned, poorly executed onboarding experience sends all the wrong signals. Conversely, a positive first impression will facilitate rapid learning and engage new starters at the outset.

The **onboarding and induction** experience can be enhanced by providing:

- a seamless online process that streamlines contract signing, policy review and sign-off, and provides information about the company before the new employee even starts

- a welcome communication that provides information about the candidate's first day – what to expect, transport and parking options, who to ask for upon entry, dress code, and what paperwork to bring

- a site tour and full safety briefing

- having all the tools necessary to do the job available on their first day (hardware, software, security access, email and calendar, and so on)

- tailored induction schedules for the candidate's first few days, detailing necessary training as well as scheduled meetings with key internal and external stakeholders with whom their role interacts

- specific induction sessions, including an induction to:
  - the company (the Business Plan)
  - the culture and values (the Culture Plan)
  - the team (Team Plan and team structure)
  - the role (job description and My Plan)

- an introduction to or experience of the organisation's product or service to ensure all new team members fully understand the quality and value of what you do

- an opportunity to sit one-on-one with their manager to understand what motivates the new employee and what learning or development goals they have

- a mention in internal comms about the new starter, their name and role in the business, and a bit about them

- planned formal check-in points with their manager to review their progress and experience at several points throughout probation – ideally the one-month and three-month mark

- access to ongoing training, mentoring, coaching and feedback necessary to perform well in the role.

Gallup research demonstrates that employees who strongly agree they have a clear plan for their professional development are 3.5 times more likely to strongly agree that their onboarding process was exceptional.

Probation is an important stage in the employee lifecycle to ensure fit – both for the employee and for the business. Where the fit is not right, their transition and experience out of the business should continue to align with your organisational values. Where the employee is consistently performing to the standard expected, the completion of probation is a milestone well worth celebrating.

Perform and develop

To effectively support performance and development, people leaders provide clarity and direction by setting SMART goals in partnership with employees which clearly align that individual's KPIs to the organisational strategy and culture priorities. (Flip back to chapter 7 to revisit the SMART goal system and some tweaks I suggest making to it.)

The employee **perform and develop** experience can be enhanced by providing:

- excellent training and development experiences, including formal training, mentoring, and on-the-job stretch assignments

- people leadership inductions and leadership development initiatives (including 360-degree feedback) that develop leaders' capabilities

- team strategy and planning workshops to set team goals, targets and project plans

- annual performance reviews to objectively assess performance, development and behaviour and re-set annual goals

- regular work-in-progress meetings and/or monthly one-on-ones with leaders to review goals, give feedback and provide coaching

- regular communication forums with the CEO and senior team to create context, meaning and connection to the organisation vision and mission

- visibility on results through dashboards and reports to stay informed of company progress

- fair and swift disciplinary action with team members who consistently underperform (despite coaching) and/or breach values and behaviours.

Gallup research shows that employees who strongly agree they have had conversations with their manager in the last six months about their goals and successes are 2.8 times more likely than other employees to be engaged.

Reward and recognise

Reward and recognition is how people are acknowledged and thanked for their efforts and contributions. Reward and recognition is also a key strategy to changing or reinforcing a culture – by demonstrating what is important, and rewarding employees accordingly.

People can be rewarded and recognised using a mix of extrinsic and intrinsic motivators. Extrinsic rewards are external motivators that often have a monetary value. Intrinsic rewards are activities that individuals find personally rewarding like opportunities for special projects or access to desirable learning and development opportunities. Some examples of these are listed below.

The **reward and recognition** experience can be enhanced by providing:

- supported study with funding or study leave to complete qualifications or necessary accreditation, external training, professional coaching, study tours or secondment opportunities

- access and introduction to professional networks or mentors that advance careers

- earned innovation time in the week – a strategy leveraged first by 3M – where employees dedicate 15% of their time to work on innovation projects of their choice

- team awards nights and award ceremonies for exceptional performance and contributions to the culture

- additional leave, leave without pay, or extended leave opportunities

- extra perks like free parking, concierge, travel lounge access, vouchers (the list is endless here)

- gifts as thank-yous for milestones such as one-year, five-year and 10-year tenure with the organisation

- team celebration lunches, team development days, or team retreats.

Engage and retain

Retaining talent has surpassed attracting talent as the number one priority for People & Culture Directors, as reported in the Great Place to Work study 2019. Engaging and retaining people means having options to balance the needs of individuals with the needs of the business. Many individuals will forego larger salaries for a workplace where they feel more connected to a shared purpose and values; and where they can achieve a better work–life integration.

The employee **engage and retain** experience can be enhanced by providing:

- flexible and equal opportunity workplaces, with options for flexible hours, part-time hours, and job-share options

- annual salary benchmarking to ensure that the team are remunerated to at least meet or exceed industry standard

- options to buy shares or earn shares in the business based on performance and tenure

- bonus incentives for achievement of business and individual KPIs leveraging fair and equitable review systems

- health and wellness programs to support mental, emotional, and physical wellbeing

- onsite childcare, subsidised childcare and paid parental leave

- referral bonus as a key attraction tool

- celebration of personal milestones such as birthdays, weddings, births

- social events including Christmas parties, Friday night drinks, trivia nights, BBQs, family days

- opportunities to meaningfully engage with the customer, community, suppliers, or environment in activities that add value, such as volunteer work or special projects.

Transition and exit

The ultimate reward and recognition is promotion and transition to roles that employees aspire to, earning them more respect, autonomy, influence, and earning power.

Exit is also an important milestone that determines whether the employee remains an advocate for the organisation.

The employee **transition and exit** experience can be enhanced by providing:

- talent programs and career conversations that fast-track advancement

- internal promotion policies that promote hiring from within

- regular workforce planning discussions

- internal communications about new recruitment opportunities, team changes, promotions, and exits that keep people informed of internal movements and encourage them to apply for internal roles they aspire towards

- handover conversations between managers of the employee transitioning; closing out of existing performance and development plans and resetting new plans relevant for the new role

- formal letters confirming the new role, salary and any relevant benefits as well as the official start date

- exit interviews and team farewells that befit the individual and their reason for exit

- farewell gifts thanking people for their tenure and contribution.

> Being able to demonstrate career growth and advancement within your own organisation is a key retention tool.

When an employee is ready for transition into a new role or promotion, they are inducted into their new role and the cycle repeats again. They may encounter several such cycles before they exit your organisation.

One of my old colleagues at Swisse, Lisa Calderone, used to say to me, 'Love them on the way out, Steph!' Loving people on the way out ensures that the employee experience remains positive well beyond tenure; and these people remain advocates of your employer brand.

BUILDING YOUR CULTURE PLAN

A Culture Plan is simply a plan on a page. It's a double-sided A4 document that clearly outlines how you honour your values and look after your employees in the pursuit of your company mission.

A Culture Plan is not one-size-fits-all. Implementing any one of the aforementioned initiatives targeted at enhancing the employee experience requires a planned and coordinated approach.

Different organisations leverage different strategies depending on their available budget and the prevailing priorities of their workforces. The process described in this section on how to build your Culture Plan provides some clear pointers for how you can highlight the great stuff your organisation already does in building a positive workplace culture, as well incorporating what your people would most value.

The following images show how I suggest organisations present their Culture Plans. The two sides of the page present us with an opportunity to zoom in from the big-picture view to a narrow, detailed view.

The front page details the company purpose, culture goal and targets; values and goals for each stage of the employee lifecycle (or employee experience goals). The back page describes the various culture initiatives that will deliver on stated goals.

Let's take a look at how to pull this information together for your organisation.

The front page

The front page should clearly state your purpose, culture goal and targets, values and employee experience goals.

Purpose

Include your purpose – your 'why, how and what' – in a prominent position on the page. Your purpose clearly communicates to all stakeholders the value you add in your chosen market.

Representing your 'why' again in the centre of the Culture Plan demonstrates that purpose is a core driver in how your company engages with employees.

Culture goal and targets

Like any plan, the Culture Plan needs to have a clear and measurable goal that states what the plan is designed to achieve. The mission of a Culture Plan is typically to create a high-performance workplace culture that fosters achievement of an organisation's purpose and strategy.

Setting measurable targets is crucial for knowing whether your plan is making an impact. Typically, the outcome of a positive culture is a highly engaged workforce who understand their drivers of performance. Engaged people do three things:

1. they **say** good things about the company

2. they want to **stay**

3. they **strive** to achieve high performance.

To measure engagement, adopt the services of a reputable provider such as Gallup or Culture Amp so that your engagement survey data can be compared to industry averages.

The Culture Plan: front

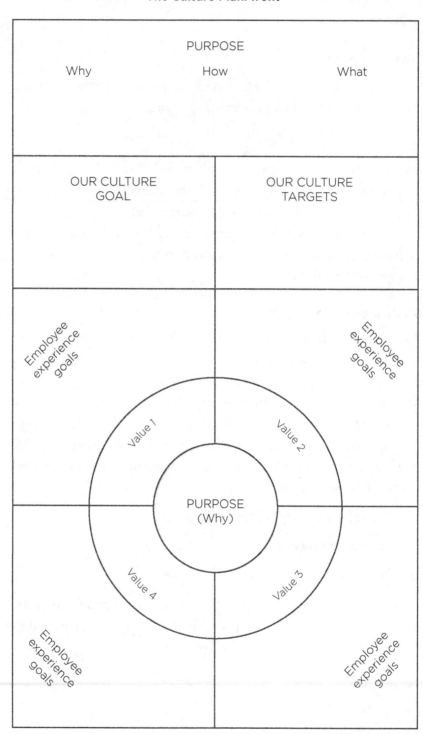

The Culture Plan: back

Value 1

GOAL
   Initiatives
GOAL
   Initiatives
GOAL
   Initiatives

Value 2

GOAL
   Initiatives
GOAL
   Initiatives
GOAL
   Initiatives

Value 3

GOAL
   Initiatives
GOAL
   Initiatives
GOAL
   Initiatives

Value 4

GOAL
   Initiatives
GOAL
   Initiatives
GOAL
   Initiatives

Other people and culture measures you may want to track and measure with a Culture Plan include:

- turnover

- safety incidents

- workcover claims

- sick leave

- recruitment time-to-hire (that is, how many weeks it takes to fill new roles)

- average team performance ratings

- percentage of internal versus external hires.

Values

Values circle your purpose. The template pictured above is for an organisation with four organisational values; however, simply adjust placement if your organisation has more or fewer values.

Employee experience goals

The employee experience goals are statements that capture the nature of the experiences employees will have at each stage of their employment lifecycle.

Matching company values to stages of the employee lifecycle by creating goals for employee experience is a simple process of linking each value to each stage.

For example, a company I worked with had four values which they made memorable by representing them with the acronym LIFE:

- Love

- Innovation

- Family

- Excellence.

Their employee experience goals for each of these pillars are shown in the table below.

Employee experience goals

Values	Employee experience goals
Love	Outstanding benefits
	Industry benchmark remuneration
	Reward and recognition programs
Innovation	Career progression opportunities
	Developing skills to perform to the highest industry standards
	Developing leadership skills to sustain a happy, productive team culture
Family	Celebrating together
	Staying connected and informed
	Caring for our health and wellbeing
Excellence	Streamlined onboarding and induction
	Regular goal-setting, feedback and review of performance
	Clearly defined roles and responsibilities

Can you see how the values here have been aligned to initiatives targeted at improving the employee experience at various stages of the employee lifecycle?

- 'Love' goals were designed to enhance the *reward and recognition* experience.
- 'Innovation' goals were designed to enhance the *performance and development* and *transition* experiences.

- 'Family' goals were designed to enhance the *engage and retain* initiatives.

- 'Excellence' goals were designed to enhance the *onboard and induct* and *perform and develop* experiences.

The back page

The back page is a showcase of all the initiatives designed to engage and enable your people and achieve your employee experience goals.

Initiatives are the ways you engage employees at each stage of the employee lifecycle. They are stated in SMART ways so that we can quantifiably measure whether they have been achieved or not.

An example is provided below.

Employee engagement initiatives

	Love
Outstanding benefits	Staff discount: 50% off across all brands
	LIFE day – an additional day of leave each month
Industry benchmark remuneration	Annual salary reviews and adjustments to remain competitive with industry benchmarks
Reward and recognition programs	Monthly LIFE awards for team members spotted living the values
	$250 bonus for referring a new team member who passes probation

The greatest advantage to listing initiatives on the back page and linking them to a strategic culture goal like this is that it fosters appreciation among staff and reminds leaders of their anchor points to lift engagement in their teams. The list of culture initiatives is like the 'PR of HR'.

ENGAGING YOUR WORKFORCE IN THE CULTURE PLAN

Engaging employees in the creation of a Culture Plan is important in gaining both buy-in and clarity on what is most important to people in your context.

Not all employee benefits are created equal. Some are known to have a greater impact on engagement than others. Seek surveyed 4800 Australians and 4000 New Zealanders on their preferences for employee perks and benefits in July 2020. Their research confirmed that what will continue to count in a post-COVID era is workplace flexibility, finance contributions (including super and insurance contributions), access to additional leave, and investment in professional development. The top 10 employee benefits listed were:

1. flexible working arrangements (59%)

2. extra superannuation (35%)

3. unlimited leave (31%)

4. professional development (26%)

5. insurance/finance discounts (19%)

6. lease car (19%)

7. additional paid parental leave (17%)

8. purchase extra annual leave (15%)

9. health/wellness programs (14%)

10. free food and coffee (12%).

ASK YOUR PEOPLE WHAT THEY WANT

While this list is helpful in guiding where to start with the most important culture initiatives, don't assume you know what your people want. Invite them to contribute their ideas either in an online survey or in a brainstorming workshop. Ask them:

• What do you love most about working here?

- If our purpose is _____ what should the goal for our culture be?

- What does our business need to achieve over the next 12 months?

- What culture do we need to achieve it?

- What do our leaders need to be doing more of or less of?

- What existing team benefits do you most value?

- What new ideas do you have that could support and enhance our culture at each stage of your employee experience?

- Of those new ideas – which ones are most important to you?

As you will read in part IV of this book, communicating and embedding the Culture Plan follows the same track as the Business Plan. The Culture Plan is an active document that may be cascaded to teams and individuals via an annual and quarterly review process of strategy creation followed by strategy execution. It becomes part of your performance DNA that actively connects people to passion and ensures your business authentically lives and breathes its values.

17

Where culture often goes wrong

If you don't manage culture, culture manages you. Culture goes wrong when we:

1. think it's something HR does

2. fail to fail

3. don't hold leaders accountable to it.

Let's take a look at each of these so you can pinpoint the red flags to watch out for in your organisation.

WE THINK CULTURE IS SOMETHING HR DOES

Human Resources (HR) departments are a relic of the past. HR was viewed as an administrative function mainly responsible for payroll and staffing. But the role and influence of HR has evolved significantly as companies recognise people as a competitive advantage and culture as an intangible asset.

The 2019 edition of the Great Place to Work study highlights that, 'HR is increasingly rebranded to People and Culture (P&C) and is no longer viewed as a cost centre but rather a source of value creation'.

HR leaders are now suitably rebranded P&C leaders, and are increasingly taking seats at the executive table. According to the Great Place to Work study, the influence of P&C on the strategic direction of organisations is on the rise: '92% of P&C heads at the 50 Best Places to Work are part of the senior leadership team, up from 70% just two years ago'.

There's no doubt that P&C adds significant value. But culture is *not* just a P&C thing. Culture is a *leadership* thing.

Driving high performance is a shared responsibility between the P&C team, people leaders and employees. Like a three-legged stool, all three are key stakeholders and must work as partners in holding up a positive workplace culture.

People and Culture specialists:

- facilitate the creation and communication of Business and Culture Plans

- set up the performance review systems, tools and templates

- train leaders in how to use the systems, tools and templates

- set up training opportunities for employees to support achievement of development goals

- evaluate and report on outcomes of Culture Plan and people goals.

People leaders:

- facilitate the translation of the business and culture goals into team and individual goals

- schedule and conduct performance reviews and regular check ins

- provide feedback and coaching to support employee goal achievement

- work with P&C teams to review team performance, design team structures and provide job descriptions

- recruit new team members or promote existing team members

- honour development plans and request specific training for their people
- collate and report on team performance outcomes.

> **Employees have the most important role to play. They are responsible for driving their own careers and working at their performance edge.**

Employees are not passengers in their experience – they are active participators. Employees:

- educate themselves on the Business and Culture Plans
- set stretch performance and development goals that align with the business and allow them to leverage strengths
- regularly review and update their own job descriptions
- turn up to conversations with managers prepared with agenda items
- request training and development that will increase skills and capacities in chosen areas
- seek feedback and coaching in achievement of performance and development goals
- collate and report on individual performance outcomes.

You can lead a horse to water but you can't make it drink. P&C people contribute to creating performance systems but ownership and accountability of culture comes down to people leaders who enable their teams and individuals who drive their own careers.

WE FAIL TO FAIL

Professor Amy Edmondson is the Novartis Professor of Leadership at Harvard Business School and author of *The Fearless Organization*. By far my favourite quote from her book is that 'failing to fail is a failure'!

Professor Edmondson demonstrates that in workplaces where it's safe to learn from mistakes, people experience high degrees of psychological safety, and this is a critical cultural factor determining whether leadership and strategy will ultimately impact performance. She says psychological safety is 'a culture in which people are comfortable expressing and being themselves'.

To thrive in the new age, growth will be driven by ideas, ingenuity, collaboration. Growth will be driven by speaking up. The problem that Professor Edmondson's research revealed is that people are holding back too often. They do this because of interpersonal risk. Where interpersonal risk is high – like in the toxic and defensive cultures mentioned back in chapter 12 – the risk of being admonished or blamed for a mistake or missed opportunity causes people to withhold crucial information and this not only stifles both creativity and learning, but creates internal politics.

Professor Edmonson discovered this quite by accident in her research into medical teams, when contrary to her expectations, she found that high-performing teams reported more mistakes (such as errors on dosages or patient care procedures) than low-performing teams. Upon further investigation, she understood that high-performing teams did not actually *make* more mistakes than low-performing teams. The difference came down to the fact that high-performing teams felt safe to report mistakes so that everyone had the opportunity to learn from them. In high-performing teams, psychological safety was the mitigating factor – mistakes were seen as learning opportunities and not reasons to admonish, shame or blame. This accelerated performance for the whole group, and enabled them to deliver better patient outcomes on a host of measures. In these teams, interpersonal risk is minimised and patient outcomes are put before personal safety.

Most of the time we want to look smart, capable and helpful. We don't want to look ignorant, incompetent or disruptive by asking questions, admitting to mistakes, making suggestions or questioning a plan. But we must take these risks to create value – for our customers, our teams and ourselves. If we don't take risks, we don't learn.

Psychological safety is like the fertile soil in garden. Without it, no seeds will take root and grow.

The Swisse team called mistakes *Learning, Growing and Improving* opportunities, or 'LGI moments!' People were given permission to learn, and this made everyone more receptive to feedback and coaching.

In high-performance cultures, leaders both destigmatise failure and learn how to positively respond to failure. According to Professor Edmonson: 'Because fear of reporting failure is such a key indicator of an environment with low levels of psychological safety, how leaders present the role of failure is essential.' Hence my new favourite catch cry – failing to fail is a failure!

WE DON'T HOLD LEADERS ACCOUNTABLE

In workplaces, we take our behavioural cues from our leaders.

Modelling behaviour starts at the very top and cascades through the entire organisation.

We constantly take note of the subtle dance of social interactions between leaders and their teams. Human Synergistics calls this the *leadership – culture – performance* connection. There is a circular relationship between leadership and culture: leaders influence culture, and culture influences leadership. The interplay between them drives performance.

In their analysis of five Australian companies, Human Synergistics researcher Quentin Jones and his colleagues confirmed that the contributions of CEOs were critical in supporting successful culture transformation programs. Importantly, CEOs demonstrated a personal commitment through 360-degree feedback and serious ongoing efforts to change their behaviour.

Gordon Cairns was the CEO at Lion Nathan at the time, one of the organisations participating in the study. He is quoted in their research as saying:

> Most people (leaders) recognise that you can't get good results without a great culture, but they think that culture is something that's out there and doesn't start with them, that's the difficulty ... There is no

such thing as 'the company'. The company is individuals. And it's individuals that have to change.

Leadership is the greatest culture lever. To build a high-performance culture, leaders must be made accountable to their behaviours with quantifiable feedback and measurement tools that raise self-awareness and develop leaders' emotional intelligence.

One charismatic executive I worked with was well known in his business to be hot tempered and reactive. When under stress, this individual was known to yell down the phone, bang things on his desk, slam doors, and openly berate members of his team. When calm, he was completely the opposite – lovable, humorous, generous. However, the business was growing in complexity and unfortunately his 'Jekyll and Hyde' act was emerging far too regularly. The situation was untenable.

His CEO reached out and we agreed to conduct 360-degree feedback using a validated psychometric tool and emotional intelligence coaching. The feedback was confronting – there were vast gaps between the executive's self-ratings and the ratings from others on a number of key dimensions. He was genuinely shocked at this – he had thought he was managing his stress quite well and hadn't realised that his behaviour has having a negative impact on his team.

The executive undertook coaching to help him recognise when stress levels were rising, and to adopt tactics to both build his resilience and better manage his emotional reactions.

He completed the 360-degree EI assessment six months later – and was encouraged to observe his scores all moving in the right direction. As a bonus, he started to notice positive changes to his health and in relationships with his family.

For there to be a high degree of congruence between espoused and lived values, leaders must be made accountable. It is their behaviour that ultimately drives culture. Employees know their organisation is serious about culture only when they see leaders actively working on their own behaviour.

HOLDING PEOPLE ACCOUNTABLE WITHOUT BREAKING PSYCHOLOGICAL SAFETY

Being able to safely hold people accountable to mistakes and failures, particularly preventable ones, is an art.

Professor Edmonson defines three different types of failure:

1. **Preventable failure:** mistakes that could have been avoided had established processes been followed.

2. **System failure:** unanticipated errors or breakdowns due to new or unique circumstances.

3. **Innovation failure:** an unsuccessful trial as part of the innovation process.

Preventable failures are often the most common that leaders encounter, and consequently generate the most frustration. Responding productively to preventable failures with a patient, calm and rational approach goes a long way towards fostering a team where psychological safety is a key feature.

Professor Edmonson's suggested productive ways of responding to 'preventable' failure, along with my suggestions for the language you can adopt to address them, are:

1. **Training:** 'Do you need me to take you through how to update your KPI achievement in the online performance platform again?', 'What is it that you're not understanding?', 'What do you expect is a reasonable way to prepare for these sessions?'

2. **Retraining:** 'You're about half-way there. But this part is still missing – did you realise there is still a gap in your preparation? Do you need me to explain again?'

3. **Process improvement:** 'Talk me through your process. Maybe we can find a better way?'

4. **System redesign:** 'Perhaps this process is not enough or out of date ... should we come up with a new way?'

5. **Sanctions:** If repeated or otherwise blameworthy actions are found.

If sanctions are required, I suggest using the AID Model, which we discussed in chapter 8, to give constructive feedback. For example:

Action: 'When you don't come prepared to these meetings ... '

Impact: ' ... the impact is that (any one of):

- Our meetings take longer than they need to/are inefficient.
- I don't feel confident you have grasped our new standards.
- We don't have access to up-to-date performance information as a management team and therefore can't make decisions.
- You are not meeting the requirements of your role – which may impact on the speed of your career progression.
- You impact on your own reputation for reliability within the team.
- Your incentives and rewards are at risk if this continues.
- The project or deliverable is at risk if we don't focus on it.

Desired outcome: 'Next time it'd be better if ... you prepare adequately/put your hand up if you need help/more training/more time/think the meeting needs to be rescheduled.'

In more serious and ongoing cases, where clear violations of standards are demonstrated, Professor Edmonson supports a firm but fair approach:

'Yes, firing can sometimes be an appropriate and productive response to a blameworthy act ... psychological safety is reinforced rather than harmed by fair, thoughtful responses to potentially dangerous, harmful, or sloppy behaviour.'

Part III summary

- Inclusive and adaptive workplace cultures create the context in which everybody lifts to bring their best game. Culture drives engagement and ignites passion for your purpose.

- Culture is the result of shared values, norms and expectations that drive behaviour at work.

- People's behaviour matters. You may have the world's greatest product and go-to-market strategy, but if you do not have a culture that emphasises constructive behaviour and healthy functioning of the human system, the business will only ever perform at an average or sub-average level.

- The Culture System is your process for ensuring that you live and honour your values and maintain the engagement and wellbeing of your people.

- The Culture System involves the creation and communication of:

  - your purpose beyond profit – how you add value to all stakeholders of your business

  - your values and behaviours – how you behave in the pursuit of your purpose or company mission

  - a Culture Plan that clearly communicates how you live your values at each stage of the employee lifecycle.

- Progressive CEOs understand that culture and strategy are equally important in driving performance outcomes, and that leaders connect people to a shared system of values and beliefs.

- Your purpose is your primary reason for being. To truly ignite passion, share how your business serves a genuine purpose beyond profit.

- Purpose-driven organisations take a balanced view of success and measure their worth in terms of value-add across multiple stakeholder groups.

- Purpose statements, when stated simply and uniquely, are powerful tools that build passion and energy for your brand. Good purpose statements are:
  - short and sharp
  - specific and clear
  - aspirational and enduring.

- Purpose includes your *why, how and what*:
  - why you exist
  - how you are unique
  - what you do.

- Values provide an essential moral compass, defining how you behave in the pursuit of your company mission.

- Values are markers for people, calling those who share similar values, who will be most likely to be successful and flourish in your operating context. Values indicate what we deem as positive, what we recognise and what we reward.

- To empower people to have behaviour conversations, it is necessary to describe the behaviours that align with company core values.

- No-one, no matter how effective their results, is above the company culture. Values are truly put to the test when employers are faced with a decision to keep or let go of their 'brilliant jerks' – people who are very talented at what they do, but don't support others around them or demonstrate the company's values.

- The Culture Plan is a culture asset that demonstrates, at a glance, how your company honours its values in the ways it deals with employees at each stage of the employee lifecycle, including:
  - attract and select
  - onboard and induct
  - perform and develop

- reward and recognise
- engage and retain
- transition and exit.
- The Culture Plan is a two-sided A4 document:
  - The front page details the culture goal and targets; company purpose; values and goals for each stage of the employee lifecycle (or employee experience goals).
  - The back page describes the various culture initiatives that will deliver on stated goals.
- While research shows that some employee benefits are consistently voted as more important, engaging employees in the creation of a Culture Plan is important in both gaining both clarity on priorities and buy-in.
- Culture goes wrong when people:
  - think it's something HR does
  - fail to fail
  - don't hold leaders accountable to it.

Part IV

The Strategy System

'Simplicity is the ultimate sophistication.'

Leonardo da Vinci

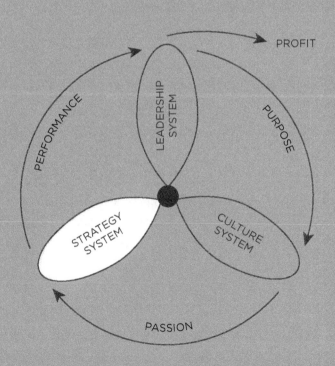

THE INNOVATION MAZE

A team of 10 executives are positioned down one end of a 9 × 6 grid taped to the floor by masking tape. They are on the clock – five minutes into a 20-minute team leadership experiential exercise called the Innovation Maze, one of my favourites from Stephen Kaagan's *Leadership Games*. Their task is to move all team members from one side of the grid to the other, stepping on an invisible path.

One person has the map showing the correct way, but the only way she can communicate with the team is to hit a bell each time the person on the maze steps on a 'wrong' square. She is not allowed to show them the map or give them any signals other than the bell.

They must play by the rules:

- Only one person at a time is allowed on the maze.

- When the team are 'innovating' – stepping on the maze – they are not allowed to talk to each other; they may only gesture and point.

- If they want to talk, they must all be behind the start line as a group.

- There are no other resources – no paper, pencils, or ways of recording progress through the maze.

Their only way of finding the path across the maze is by trial and error – by stepping out and discovering the 'right' squares across to the other side each time there is no bell. They win if every team member finds their way across within the timeframe.

There are so many lessons we can learn from this activity, but the reason I am sharing this story here is to demonstrate how strategy happens.

When I run this activity, most teams jump straight into action and one person, usually the most competitive, steps onto the maze without consultation. Progress is always slow initially because the maze moves in unpredictable ways. They don't have a plan, they just get out there and try it.

It's not until I apply time pressure and tell the group they only have 10 minutes left that they usually change tack and remember that they can talk to each other if they all get behind the line. This is where they start to talk about their strategy. They discuss what's not working. They figure out a system. Then they get back out there and try again.

Following this pattern, teams work out that periods on the maze, interspersed with brief periods of discussion back behind the line, is the best way to facilitate rapid learning and engage the whole group in the exercise. They naturally fall into a rhythm of planning and execution, with more time overall in execution than in planning.

The teams that do the best delegate roles – maze finders who rotate on and off; spotters positioned at different points along the grid. They also work out communication systems – signals for 'yes', 'no', and 'I don't know!' The teams that are *exceptional* at this delegate roles based on strengths – the quick and tactile movers are on the maze; those with good visual memory are positioned at points to remember the path; natural leaders observe the whole dynamic and decide when it's time to get back behind the line and discuss a new plan if the old one is not working.

This game is a perfect example of how strategy actually happens.

18

The value of strategy

At its most basic level, a strategy is a plan to realising a vision. But plans are limited – we can only form them based on the experiences and inputs we have at the time. The more information and experience we gain, the better our plans become. Plans are simply ideas that get you moving on a path towards your vision; *action* is where you learn the true nature of the game. Plans must be put to the test; and the quicker they can be tested, the more people learn, and the more effective their strategy creation process becomes.

Strategic planning is like building a bridge. As you build, you learn about the water currents; river traffic; the strength and pace of the men and women building. Your ability to build that bridge gets better as you learn and apply the process, until you finally reach the other side (or meet in the middle). At which point you either sell the bridge, split the profit and buy a nice little townhouse; or mortgage your bridge to build another one! The metaphor goes on ...

Strategy is enhanced when it's treated as a dynamic process of creation followed by execution.

When we play the game of strategy, we play a game of four quarters. The quarters could be spread over a financial year; a month; a day; or a 20-minute rapid process.

However long the timescale, the balance of time spent in creation vs execution should be about 80/20:

• 20% strategy creation

• 80% strategy execution.

**Strategy creation to strategy execution –
a game of four quarters**

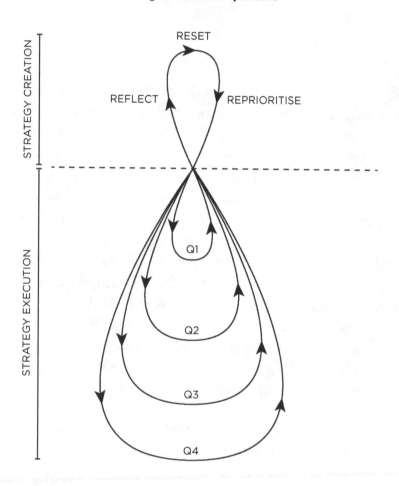

Each time we take a swing at strategy creation, we reflect on our learned experience; reset our approach; and reprioritise our actions. This is a perpetual process, and each time we play the game we get better at it so that by the time we hit the fourth quarter we are running at double the speed.

Back on The Innovation Maze, most teams make it across around the 20-minute mark. I always run a debrief asking the group to reflect on:

- What did you do well?

- What could you have done better?

- How is this like work?

- If you had your chance to do this again, how would you do it differently?

Teams talk about how they would spend more time planning up front, delegate roles appropriate to strengths, ensure all team members are engaged and no-one is sidelined, agree to regroup when the same mistake is made twice, and above all help the 'innovators' cutting the path through the maze – their role is the most important to success for the whole.

Then I give them an option to put their theories to the test: run the activity again, with a new path but only half the time. Most teams take up the option, and over 90% are successful in completing within 10 minutes. How? Because they have learned the 'strategy creation' to 'strategy execution' process.

A SYSTEMS VIEW OF STRATEGY

If we take an open-systems view as described in chapter 2, where organisations are systems that exist via exchange with the environment through an import, conversion, export process; strategy is a representation of the way links are made between the inside and the outside of the organisation. (Flip back to chapter 2 for more on the import, conversion, export process.)

These links can be made in a planned way or in an emergent way:

- **Planned** strategy uses formal Strategic Planning tools like SWOT, ·or the Kaplan & Norton Balanced Scorecard.

- **Emergent** strategy is a realisation of patterns that have emerged from the past.

Both have validity as part of a Strategic Planning process, and in fact when deliberately used together are more powerful.

Professor Henry Mintzberg introduced the concept of emergent strategy – 'strategy that emerges over time as intentions collide with and accommodate a changing reality'. Much like the maze innovators, emergent strategy evolves as plans are tested, reflected upon, and then used to remodel actions and tactics moving forward. The emphasis is on learning and responding; both shaping and being shaped by external forces in the operating context.

For example – a planned company strategy for growth may involve investing $1 million to build up stock holdings and speed up customer delivery and response times. However, when the COO moves to execute this plan with her suppliers, real limitations in the supply chain prevent the plan from being possible. Does this mean the strategy was ill conceived? No, it means that a good idea, put to the test, failed. This is just part of trial and error. The COO must now ideate another way to speed customer response times or improve the customer experience in the short term; while continuing to work with suppliers on options to boost their production capability.

Taking the systems view further, strategy also represents the way links are made internally, between the various sub-components of an organisation. Strategy is not just reserved for boards and executive teams. Strategy creation and execution happens at the organisational level, the team level, and the individual level.

The process of strategy creation and execution empowers each role to dynamically interact with other roles in the achievement of shared objectives. Managers operate at the boundary, supporting individuals to set individual performance goals and empowering them to find innovative ways to execute their plans. In turn, individual insights gained through direct experience with customers and internal teams inform the whole system where strategies are successful and where they need to be altered.

The survival and adaptation of the organisation depends on having diversity within the system to effectively anticipate and respond to dynamic changes in the operating context. *Diversity* is a key word here – a variety of viewpoints, experiences, backgrounds and ideas adds texture and depth to a strategy-creation process. This increases the organisation's competitive advantage – but only if diversity can be harnessed and shared. Strategy creation is a process of listening to different viewpoints and extracting the simple truths that everyone is willing to agree on. This is why a coaching approach is important; leaders who coach ask questions of the group and listen to the answers, searching for the shared truths that a combination of perspectives and experiences may reveal.

Ultimately, while strategy can be viewed as a plan to realise a vision, it is more than that. It's an essential process that drives engagement, facilitates rapid learning and adaptation, activates team intelligence, and aligns effort towards a singular purpose.

Strategies act like signposts. They tell people what direction to head and how to safely get there.

> **A good Strategic Plan aligns teams and enables them to journey with maximum efficiency in formation towards a shared vision.**

THE STRATEGY LADDER

The key to realising the full value from your strategy and gaining alignment across a whole organisation is to get it out of people's heads and onto a page to make it not just clear, but also actionable.

The strategy ladder describes the stages of strategy creation. Strategy can be *invisible* (either non-existent or only inside people's heads) to *actionable* – clear, concise and able to be implemented.

The presence (or absence) of strategy impacts how teams act and ultimately the level of alignment in your business.

The strategy ladder

Strategy	Focus on	Behaviour	Ratio % aligned to % misaligned
Actionable	Achieving	Implement	90:10
Clear	Accepting	Plan	60:40
Complicated	Questioning	Compete	50:50
Outdated	Assuming	Guess	40:60
Invisible	Reacting	Drown	10:90

Let's consider each of these, starting from the bottom.

Invisible

In some companies, there is no visible strategy at all. The company is caught in a **reactive** cycle; responding to their market or to the actions of competitors. Teams in these companies often **drown** under competing priorities or infighting because there is no focused direction for their effort and energy; and they end up taking direction from people with the most influence or power in the system. This results in significant misalignment – where teams have no access to organisation-wide objectives and may even inadvertently work against each other.

Outdated

If strategy creation is only treated as an annual event and rarely revisited at the organisation, team and individual level, very quickly it loses relevance and becomes outdated. While an outdated strategy is better than no strategy at all (it at least gives the team signposts as to what the CEO is looking at), it requires that teams must make **assumptions** and play **guesswork** in deciding how to prioritise their time and direct their efforts. This also results in misalignment between teams; albeit less than that found in situations where the strategy is invisible.

> **Never before have so many companies been faced with outdated Strategic Plans at such scale than as when coronavirus hit the global economy.**

Very quickly, many Strategic Plans devised under entirely different economic conditions became irrelevant, as companies went into survival mode. Time taken between old strategy becoming outdated and new strategy emerging put many teams into holding patterns – simply responding to the greatest perceived need of the day. CEOs who rapidly realigned their people on a new strategy were able to adapt and, in some cases, capitalise on new opportunities (for example, switching operations to hand sanitiser or personal protective equipment manufacturing, scaling online, focusing on delivering exceptional customer value to maintain customers). As the world started to tentatively re-open for business, the CEOs who responded with new re-emergence strategies were able to switch back to pre-COVID offerings or launch new services that were more relevant in the new economy.

If your strategy is outdated, your people work in outdated ways. Every time a team revisits strategy, things become clearer – some things that were considered high priority three months ago are no longer as important. Perhaps the market shifted, an unanticipated crisis occurred, or some other opportunity took greater precedence.

Updating a plan does not necessarily mean wholesale change – it just means iteration. Adjustments and clarifications are made so that it maintains relevance and meaning in the minds of the people executing the plan.

Complicated

Complicated strategies cause people to **question** their significance and **compete** for resources. Complicated and detailed strategies are just too hard to follow. Too much detail can be as debilitating as none at all. Humans only have the mental capacity to hold 7 +/– 2 items in short-term memory at any one time. More than nine items and we cannot remember them let alone effectively communicate, measure or track them.

A common process that some organisations follow is to ask their senior leaders to come up with their own Strategic Plan for their own areas. While this is an empowering approach, it can result in misalignment. Without a shared strategy for the whole organisation to form the stem from which all other planning happens, we run the risk of fostering competing priorities and internal competition for resources. In these scenarios, the loudest voice or the individual with the most positional power often wins the attention of the CEO and therefore the support. What we don't want are internal winners and losers. We just want winners.

Complicated strategies give teams only a 50/50 chance of aligning on organisational priorities.

Clear

A clear strategy is one that people **accept** and effectively **plan** to execute. Clear plans use plain language to articulate what drives business performance. You don't need a business degree to interpret them. They have memorable one-liners that effectively tell the story about the company purpose, vision and strategic direction.

Clear plans result in stronger alignment between teams, where teams work collaboratively on projects in planned and structure ways at least 60% of the time.

Actionable

An actionable strategy is one that teams focus on **achieving** by **implementing** clear actions that drive results. Actionable plans clearly articulate not just the why and what, but the how. That is, if you're asking the Head of Sales to grow sales from $50 million to $60 million in the next 12 months, actionable plans articulate how teams must collaborate to achieve growth goals. They include goals and targets – as well as priorities and initiatives that teams work together to achieve; in simple measurable terms and plain language. Actionable strategy fosters over 90% alignment between teams, because it clearly directs and inspires actions that drive results.

***

Where do you sit on the strategy ladder? What would it do for your business if your people were more aligned; working consistently towards the same goals in planned and coordinated ways?

The Strategy System takes strategy from being invisible (inside your head) to actionable, resulting in 90%+ alignment.

Implementing a system for strategy allows your organisation to remain agile and responsive to shifting market trends while also being focused on long-term aspirations that closely align with your purpose and values.

A clear and actionable strategy delivers another major advantage: it empowers decision making. For Radek Sali, the Swisse Wellness Business Plan pushed accountability down the line:

> It went away from one person driving a group of implementers to people being empowered to make decisions and being able to make those decisions without me, or whoever had been in charge of Swisse in the room, and know the parameters of what would deliver success.

The Strategy System aligns your whole team on the same page.

19

Introducing
The Strategy System

The Strategy System is your process for strategy creation and execution that ensures your organisation remains adaptive and responsive in your chosen market.

The Strategy System aligns the whole team to work collaboratively. It involves:

- creating a one-page Business Plan that is clear and actionable

- cascading goals through to teams and individuals through alignment sessions

- evaluating performance to review progress and to reflect on opportunities for continuous improvement.

The Strategy System fosters transparency and rapid adaptation, resulting in:

- clarity of purpose

- goal alignment

- leadership accountability.

The Strategy System

The one-page plan that is created through this process should be reviewed annually but visited quarterly as part of your business planning and budget cycle.

The front page outlines your purpose, values, vision, pillars, goals and key performance indicators (KPIs). The back page lists the priorities driving outcomes in each pillar and the teams within the business who must collaborate to deliver these projects.

Each team member's KPIs and priorities cascade directly from this plan, and each quarter their progress is tracked in team planning workshops to reflect, reset and reprioritise for the quarter ahead. This process allows the business to remain agile, adjusting the plan as the market shifts while remaining steadfast in your company mission.

The process allows the whole team to have input into the strategy and how they can achieve their own plans. This creates engagement, ownership and accountability throughout the organisation.

Each quarter, the CEO reports back to the business on performance against the goals and targets outlined in the Business Plan; sharing achievements against each pillar and highlighting individuals who demonstrated outstanding effort for reaching key milestones. He or she also communicates their perspective on focus areas for the upcoming quarter.

HOW THE STRATEGY SYSTEM FUELS PERFORMANCE

Strategy fuels performance by ensuring all team members set and are accountable to results.

By implementing a cyclical process involving strategy creation; cascading and alignment; and evaluation and review; businesses create teams that are clear on how their work impacts performance outcomes and how they can adjust their priorities to impact results.

There are numerous advantages to implementing a system for strategy:

- The team becomes inspired by the bigger picture of the organisation and the role they play in achieving great things.

- Everyone can talk about strategy in simple terms and in everyday language, using it to guide daily prioritisation and decision making.

- Individuals learn about how their day-to-day performance habits impact results.

- Individuals are educated in the indicators of success, including revenue, profit, cost levers, market value and the company position relative to competitors.

- Individuals start to think and behave like business owners, making decisions that are in the best interests of the organisation.

- In times of change and market volatility (like a global pandemic), a strategy system enables teams to pivot, because the process of strategy creation, cascading, and evaluating is well rehearsed.

20

Your Business Plan – a strategy on a page

Have you ever watched birds flying in formation? The symmetric V shape is adopted by many migratory bird species, including geese, swans and ducks. The V formation is more than just a beautiful sight to behold; it serves two important purposes. First, it reduces wind resistance, which conserves the birds' energy. Each bird takes a turn being at the front, falling back when they get tired. Second; it allows them to easily keep track of every bird in the group, and is thought to assist with communication and coordination. Fighter pilots use this formation for the same reason.

Like birds flying in formation, a one-page Business Plan enables your people to efficiently and effectively migrate from where you are now to where you need to be. It translates your vision into clear and measurable action.

It's not enough to just have a highly engaged, positive culture filled with smart, capable people. To harness your team's collective potential, you must have a single source of the truth which is the base from which all other activities cascade.

EVOLUTION OF THE ONE-PAGE PLAN

The one-page plan method has been evolving over the last two decades. In 1996, Robert Kaplan and David Norton introduced the concept of The Balanced Scorecard. The Balanced Scorecard takes a balanced approach to organisational performance measurement by setting goals, measures, targets and initiatives across four pillars: Financial, Customer, Internal Business Process, and Learning & Growth.

By taking a balanced approach, financial and non-financial measures link together to paint the picture for what is strategically important. Scorecards are cascaded from the company-wide level to teams and individuals, and this process provides clarity to every individual about how their role adds value. Because every person has a role to play in driving all strategic pillars, this process actively works against the silo mentality, encouraging collaboration across departments in the achievement of shared goals.

Verne Harnish, founder of Entrepreneurs' Organization (EO) and Gazelles, and author of *Scaling Up*, took this thinking a step further in the 2010s. He showed us how to take this balanced view concept and put it on a single page, with the goal of keeping your Strategic Plan easy to communicate and clearly actionable.

Since then, several strategy systems using the one-page-plan concept have emerged from thought leaders, including Gino Wickman and Jeroen De Flander. Each system has its own variations and accompanying tools.

The Strategy System presented in this book presents another one-page plan. The unique differentiator of this version is that it aligns with the systems for leadership and culture we looked at earlier in this book as part of an overall high-performance system.

I encourage you, dear reader, to research broadly and make an informed choice about the approach that will best suit your business. Whichever strategy creation process you choose to adopt, the real power of this method is in your process for engaging and aligning your whole team; empowering leaders at every level to be accountable; and staying relevant and adaptive in your chosen market.

> **A one-page plan that is communicated well and embedded at both team and individual level is a proven method to align the whole team to work collaboratively.**

BUILDING YOUR BUSINESS PLAN – A STRATEGY ON A PAGE

Just like the Culture Plan has two sides allowing for narrowing in from big picture to detailed view, the Business Plan has the same structure.

The front page of the plan details the purpose, values, vision, pillars, goals and KPIs.

The back page of the plan details the priority projects to achieve goals and KPIs, the departments contributing, and the leaders responsible.

Each component of the Business Plan is represented in the diagrams on the following pages.

Business Plan: front

PURPOSE		
Why	How	What

VALUES

VISION		
1 year	3 years	10 years

FINANCE PILLAR	CUSTOMER PILLAR
Goal	Goal
KPIs – – – –	KPIs – – – –
PEOPLE PILLAR	**PROCESS PILLAR**
Goal	Goal
KPIs – – – –	KPIs – – – –

Business Plan: back

1 YEAR	DEPARTMENTS							LEADER ACCOUNT-ABLE
	Pr	S	M	O	Pe	F	C	
FINANCE PRIORITIES 1 2 3								
CUSTOMER PRIORITIES 1 2 3								
PROCESS PRIORITIES 1 2 3								
PEOPLE PRIORITIES 1 2 3								

KEY: Pr = PRODUCT | S = SALES | M = MARKETING | O = OPERATIONS | Pe = PEOPLE & CULTURE | F = FINANCE | C = CORPORATE

Let's take a look at how to pull this information together for your organisation.

The front page of your Business Plan

The front page should clearly state your purpose, values, vision and pillars, with accompanying goals and KPIs.

Purpose

Your purpose is your primary reason for being. It is the difference you make, the value you add, the change you create. Just like on the Culture Plan, your purpose – or your why, how and what – is at the forefront of your one-page Business Plan.

For more on purpose flip back to chapter 14.

Values

Values provide an essential moral compass to your business. Values exist on a one-page plan because they are ever-present and define the way you do business.

For more on how to create your values list refer back to chapter 15.

Vision

Your vision is what the world will look like when you are achieving your purpose. Jim Collins called the vision your BHAG – big hairy audacious goal. It's hairy because it's like the big monster in the room you just can't avoid looking at. It makes you feel that heady mixture of fear and exhilaration, like your life depends on conquering this beast (or making it your friend).

Visions paint the picture for a positive future and serve a very functional purpose. Whether we are conscious of it or not, we all carry around visions or mental images for our roles, our businesses, our lives. Your mental image may be vivid and colourful, or it may be cloudy and tinged. Whatever image you either consciously or sub-consciously conjure, your brain will do everything in its extraordinary power to materialise.

There is something in your brain called a reticular activating system (RAS). Your RAS is like a finely tuned detection device. If you tell it something you want or are interested in, it scans the environment for you and alerts you when that object is detected. Have you ever had the experience of deciding to buy a new car, and then you start seeing that car on the road everywhere? It's not that there are suddenly more of those cars on the road, it's just that your RAS is now noticing them. Your RAS helps you see what is right in front of you in the service of goal achievement.

By painting a clear vision for your organisation, you signal to your people what to look out for and what opportunities to seize as they present themselves.

> **Vision statements are high-level measurable statements that define what success looks like in the short, medium and long term.**

These are the towns you visit on the journey to destination 'purpose'.

Many organisations select a one-, three- and 10-year time horizon, with the one- and three-year horizons reviewed and updated annually as they progress towards the 10-year vision. Others (particularly start-ups and organisations in volatile markets) work to shorter horizons like 1, 2 and 5 years, because they cannot reliably foresee the future. In contrast, some organisations – such as climate change, mining and construction companies, or governments working on large-scale infrastructure or social change projects – work to 20-year+ time horizons. There are no hard and fast rules here – the time horizons you set will depend on what is right for the organisation and industry you are in.

For them to be meaningful, vision statements should be measurable. In her book *Prove It!*, performance measurement expert Stacey Barr recommends choosing just one or two performance measures that provide real and objective evidence that your organisation is fulfilling its mission. Revenue and profit are typical high-level performance measures, as are desired market position.

A suggested basic structure for your one-year, three-year and 10-year vision statement is:

One-year: Be top 10 XX brand in XX market

Three-year: Grow XX% year on year and maintain XX% EBITDA

10-year: Be the #1 brand in the XX market

For example:

One-year: Offer the most ethically sourced and sustainable skincare brand for 25- to 35-year-old women; with a presence in the top 3 online Australian pharmaceutical retailers

Three-year: Grow 100% year on year to become Australia's # 1 skin care brand

10-year: Be # 1 skin care brand online in the Asia Pacific and invest 1% for the planet

HOW TO CREATE A VISION STATEMENT

Crafting a vision is both a right-brain, creative thinking and left-brain, rational and structured exercise. It involves actually imagining the future – dreaming what it will look like and feel like if we are to realise our full potential, and putting measurable markers against it.

One way to create a vision statement is to bring the key people in your team or organisation together for a Dream exercise. This exercise is part of the appreciative inquiry process created by Dr David Cooperrider (2005) (we met him in chapter 15) involving guided visualisation. Here's how it works:

1. Run a short, eyes-closed meditation exercise to move the group into a relaxed state and shift their focus internally.

2. After a few minutes of settling into this comfortable, quiet space, with eyes remaining closed, ask the group to imagine they have awoken from a very deep and long sleep and it is now the year (insert your long-term horizon). You look around and (your organisation name) is very different. Your dream has become a reality and it has unfolded just as you had imagined and hoped.

3. Give the group 60 seconds to allow their internal mental images to form in this dream of the future.

4. After 60 seconds is over, invite them to work in smaller groups (pairs or threes) to discuss and document what they saw, felt and experienced during the guided visualisation.

5. Ask each group to feed back their collective dream by completing this sentence: In 10 years (assuming that is your preferred long-term horizon), we are …

6. Collate and distil everyone's sentences into a single measurable statement that captures the essence of them all.

Once you have your 10-year vision defined, work your way back to what must be achieved in the next three years, and then within the next year.

By end of this activity you should have three sentences starting with:

In 1 year, we are: _____

In 3 years, we are: _____

In 10 years, we are: _____

Pillars

Pillars are the focus areas or strategic themes that will coordinate team action towards achievement of strategic goals. They are called pillars because they form the foundational growth platform for the business. Pillars are *not* organisation departments such as Sales, Operations, and Finance. Instead, they are 'department agnostic' in that every area of the business contributes to achievement across all pillars.

The Kaplan & Norton Balanced Scorecard approach provides us with four perspectives against which we may structure strategic pillars:

1. **Finance perspective** – includes the fiscal management strategies to sustain growth and deliver a healthy bottom line that shareholders are both willing and able to support without putting too much pressure or risk on any single stakeholder.

2. **Customer perspective** – includes strategies to connect within your particular customer and market segments that will deliver specific financial returns.

3. **Internal business process perspective** – includes strategies to improve internal operational processes or integrate new processes and innovations that will impact customer satisfaction.

4. **Learning and growth perspective** – includes strategies to enhance organisational capability that sustain long-term growth through people, systems and procedures.

For simplification, I summarise these four perspectives as the **Finance**, **Customer**, **Process** and **People Pillars**.

While they are robust and broadly applicable, Kaplan & Norton (1996) recommend that 'the four perspectives should be considered a template, not a straight jacket'.

There may be other pillars that are strategically important to the company and need to be highlighted. For example, while product innovation can technically be incorporated as part of the Customer pillar; it may be separated out as its own Innovation pillar to highlight the importance of innovation to company success. In addition, while the Balanced Scorecard explicitly recognises the interests of shareholders (Finance pillar), customers (Customer pillar) and employees (People pillar), it only implicitly represents the interests of other stakeholders, including suppliers, community and the environment. If demonstrating a commitment to meeting shared interests across stakeholders is important, highlighting these stakeholders as pillars will focus the team's attention there. For example, some companies may choose to set a Sustainability, Environment or Community strategic pillar.

When choosing pillars, a general guide is to choose between three and five that provide a balanced view of the core drivers of performance. Start with the traditional Kaplan & Norton Balanced Scorecard pillars above, and then bring other pillars to the forefront or background depending on their strategic relevance to your context. Finally, give them names using your own language – language that is accessible and meaningful to you and your team.

Some examples of strategic pillars from companies I have encountered are:

Company 1: A fashion brand

Business Health

Sustainability

Community and Brand

Best Practice

People and Culture

Company 2: An FMCG company

Innovate

Grow Customer Base

Build Bench Strength

Drive Productivity

Manage Costs

Company 3: A software developer

Best People and Culture

Unrivalled Innovation

Sales Excellence

Financial Accountability

Superior Customer Experience

Company 4: A tech accessories retailer

Grow Retail

Grow Consumer Connection

Deliver Product Innovation

Find and Keep Great People

Manage Costs

Protect Market Share

Company 5: An insurer

Protect and Grow

Deliver Sustainable Financial Return

Innovate the Way We Work

Align Our Team

Company 6: A beverage company
Product
Brand
Distribution
Team

Can you see how the traditional Balanced Scorecard perspectives have been adapted and applied in each of these examples? Every business is unique, and so your strategic pillars are your way of generating an internal language around what drives the economic engine in your business. They key point here is to start with the Balanced Scorecard as a framework and then make it your own.

Goals and KPIs

Who said 'what gets measured gets managed' again? Oh yeah ... that Drucker guy! He didn't get everything wrong – some stuff he said was pretty good.

Something happens when we quantify our progress. Athletes obsess about measurements. Speed, accuracy, weight, mood. They don't obsess about measurement because they like numbers, they obsess because the mere act of watching a number and observing how it changes based on our behaviour informs decision making in crucial moments.

> **Goals are measurable statements that articulate a clear intent for driving results.**

A singular SMART goal statement should be created for each pillar – clearly communicating what success looks like in that pillar within your short-term or one-year time horizon.

KPIs are specific measures and targets that give you a definitive numerical value of success. In any business, there will be any number of different KPIs or performance markers that you can choose. The real power comes from choosing measures that matter; measures that enable goal achievement in the service of your vision and purpose. The table on the next page provides a few examples of measures you could consider. This is by no means an exhaustive list; merely a list of the more common measures I've come across from the many companies I've worked with.

Examples of measures for the Finance, Customer, Process and People pillars

Finance measures	Customer measures
• Revenue • Monthly recurring revenue • Gross profit • Net profit • COGS as a % of revenue • Marketing as a % of revenue • Labour as a % of revenue • Other expenses as a % of revenue • Cash flow • Project profitability • Capital investment targets	• Sales or growth targets for particular products, market segments, or geographical regions; such as revenue per sales person • Units sold (# items sold per week, per day, etc. ...) • Customer satisfaction targets such as Net Promoter Score (NPS), customer retention, new customer acquisition, or customer profitability • Marketing targets such as cost of customer acquisition (CAC), market share, brand awareness, customer database, social media following, media mentions
Process measures	**People measures**
• Lead times and on-time delivery • Customer issue resolution times • Defects, returns, fault counts • Forecasting accuracy • Time to market for new products • Safety incidents • Tender success rates • Project performance rates • Utilisation on projects • Revenue per employee (productivity measure)	• Retention measures: headcount, turnover • Satisfaction measures: engagement scores, climate scores • Recruitment metrics: response rates, time-to-hire • Probation metrics: percentage of candidates successfully passing probation • Performance metrics: average team performance and behaviour ratings (self and manager ratings) • Training attendance, training evaluation feedback

The KPI you identify must be something you currently have access to or can easily source. There is no point setting a measure or target for an indicator for which you have no existing data or that is too arduous and time consuming to capture. If you lack specific measures, one of your priorities will be to implement a system of measurement that will provide you with visibility on key metrics. Setting your goals and KPIs is the precursor to creating dashboards that will keep your organisation informed on performance.

The back page of your Business Plan

The back page provides visibility for the whole organisation on what the priorities are for each pillar, which departments or teams need to collaborate to achieve them, and who the leaders responsible are.

Priorities

Priorities are the initiatives, projects, activities and opportunities you will be implementing to achieve the goals and KPIs outlined for each Pillar on the front page of the plan.

As you will see in the next section on engaging your workforce in the Business Plan, a SOAR analysis (strengths, opportunities, aspirations, results) is a great way of surfacing the opportunities or aspirations that translate into priorities.

To keep the business focused and aligned, it's important to set only two or three priorities that sit within each pillar. If you have four pillars with three priorities in each, you already have 12 priorities for the next 12 months. Any more than this and the plan starts to become unwieldly. Less is definitely more when it comes to choosing your strategic priority projects. Each high-level strategic priority will have sub-priorities that will appear on Team Plans and individual plans. Keeping organisation priorities to a minimum will foster consistent language and greater alignment as they are cascaded to teams and individuals.

For this reason, your priorities need to be 'big picture' enough to require collaboration and involvement across departments to execute.

More specific or detailed priorities that are owned and led by a single department or team belong on that department's Team Plan, not the overarching Business Plan.

Departments contributing

To encourage collaboration and alignment across teams, create a series of columns that represent the structure of your organisation and indicate who must collaborate to deliver on the priority.

Traditional departments may include product development, sales, marketing, operations and customer service; plus the support functions of finance, people and culture, Information Technology (IT), and corporate governance. How your organisation is structured depends on the type of business you have, your size and complexity. Every individual in your company should be able to easily identify with a department on the back page of the plan. If you have a small organisation of less than 10 people, you do not need to identify departments but you can identify the leaders responsible.

For each priority project – identify which departments must work together to achieve this project using a basic symbol like a 'tick' or 'cross' along the row. This indicates which department must collaborate in order to achieve the priority project; and makes it necessary for those departments to factor in time and resources to contribute to the project as part of their own planning. The department who has primary accountability for the project may be highlighted with a colour or darkened background.

For example; a priority project in the Finance pillar may be:

Reduce cost of goods (COGS) to 19%

This priority is the primary responsibility of the Operations department – who has the most influence over production costs. However, it will also involve the collaboration of other departments, including

Product Development, Marketing, Finance and Corporate. On the back page of the plan, it would look like this:

FINANCE PILLAR	Product development	Sales	Marketing	Operations	People and culture	Finance	Corporate	Leader accountable
3.1 Reduce COGS to 19%.	✔		✔	✔		✔	✔	Head of Operations

Some organisations I have worked with have used the RACI framework to designate how different departments are involved in the different priorities; as either Responsible, Accountable, Consult, or Inform.

Using the same example, departments involved are Product Development (responsible), Marketing (also responsible), Operations (accountable), Finance (consult), and Corporate (inform). On the back page of the plan – it would look like this:

FINANCE PILLAR	Product development	Sales	Marketing	Operations	People and culture	Finance	Corporate	Leader accountable
3.1 Reduce COGS to 19%.	R		R	A		C	I	Head of Operations

Leader accountable

Every single priority needs an owner.

This person is ultimately accountable for driving the initiative internally. The leader accountable does not necessarily need to be responsible for executing the project, but they do need to lead it – ensure it is planned, resourced, implemented, measured and reported. The leader responsible is the go-to person for the initiative, able to answer questions, provide guidance and facilitate conversations about it. They are passionate and interested in seeing it through; and their role would naturally lend to owning it. Most often, the leader responsible is the executive or most senior person in the department; or alternatively the person best qualified and with the necessary delegated authority within the business to be empowered to execute. Achieving that priority will be a key goal on that individual's performance plan.

21

Engaging your workforce in the Business Plan

Any Founder, CEO or senior executive responsible for running a business can write a one-page plan. Gaining full alignment, clarity and accountability for that plan from the whole team is the challenge.

Creating a Business Plan is a team engagement exercise. If you want your team to have ownership, accountability and buy-in to a strategic plan, they must be involved in building it. This is true for everyone, which is why a cascading process involving Team Plan workshops and individual performance conversations gives every single person in your business the opportunity to contribute to and have ownership over, the strategy creation process.

The best way to both create and renew your one-page Business Plan to take your senior people away on an annual one- or two-day strategy retreat. Getting away from the office (or home, as is the new norm) and being together in a more relaxed space allows your key people to reconnect, reenergise and think in more creative ways. It's an important relationship-building exercise which fosters a more positive team dynamic, an absolute must in achieving aspirational goals and targets.

If you can't afford the time or investment in a two-day retreat, then at the very minimum organise an offsite one-day strategy session combined with a team dinner or social drinks. While you have less time, getting people away from their everyday workspace will still encourage them to switch gear into long-term, big-picture thinking.

Where there are barriers to in-room experiences due to geographically dispersed teams, social distancing requirements or restrictions on travel, moving your sessions to an online environment is a next best option. In these circumstances, leverage an effective communications platform and/or a skilled facilitator to enhance the experience for everyone.

Deciding who to bring into the space is very important. A basic rule is to include your top 10 people to give every voice equal weight and importance in the space. Your cascading process will ensure every person is engaged in strategy creation, so don't risk the quality of your annual strategy retreat for fear of excluding certain personalities.

In terms of timing, many groups align their strategy retreat with their annual budget cycle. Strategy directs budgeting; it informs the priorities and focal areas for reinvestment and distribution of financial resources. Some organisations re-cast strategy before the beginning of a new financial year; some do it after. Either way, choose the same month every year so that annual goals can be set. In addition, choose a month that does not clash with your busiest trade or delivery times, so that it won't put the rest of the business out or cause undue stress for your people.

PRE-WORK FOR YOUR BUSINESS PLAN

There's no doubt that strategy is a creative design process. It's like looking into a crystal ball. No-one can see the future – at best we make educated guesses.

In *The 4-Hour Work Week*, Tim Ferriss undertook an analysis using Pareto's 80/20 rule to find freedom from futility. He dissected his personal life and business through the lenses of two questions:

1. Which 20% of sources are causing 80% of my problems and unhappiness?

2. Which 20% of sources are resulting in 80% of my desired outcomes and happiness?

Tim writes, 'The goal is to find your inefficiencies in order to eliminate them and to find your strengths so you can multiply them'. In the 24 hours that followed his analysis, Tim made several difficult decisions that changed his life forever and led him to exponentially increase his wealth and live a life by design.

To support your strategy creation process, do the pre-work to inform judgement and support your best guess:

1. Get the right quantitative data in the room.

2. Get the right qualitative data in the room.

To get the right quantitative data in the room

Ask your finance people to pull together a simple spreadsheet that tracks financial performance over the last five years against:

*   revenue

*   cost of goods sold (COGS)

*   gross profit (revenue minus COGS)

*   net profit (revenue after all expenses, often reported as EBITDA)

*   breakdown of revenue and profit per product or service

*   breakdown of revenue and profit per customer segment or channel.

If you are a parent company to several businesses, you may want to look at revenue per subsidiary, and then provide these breakdowns for each subsidiary.

	Actual					Target		
	2016	2017	2018	2019	2020	2021	2022	2023
Business as a whole								
Revenue								
COGS								
Gross profit								
Net profit								
Breakdown								
Product/category view								
Product 1 revenue								
Product 1 profit								
Product 2 revenue								
Product 2 profit								
Product 3 revenue								
Product 3 profit								
Customer/channel view								
Customer 1 revenue								
Customer 1 profit								
Customer 2 revenue								
Customer 2 profit								
Customer 3 revenue								
Customer 3 profit								

Use the data generated to plot a series of graphs and answer these questions as the commentary:

- What is our current rate of growth?
- What is our current profit (gross and net)?
- What is the 80/20 in our business?
  - What 20% of sales generates 80% of revenue?
  - What 20% of problems are utilising 80% of our time?
- What are the high- versus low-profit generating activities? What is the strategic value of our low-profit activities? If there is no strategic value to low-profit activities, what can we stop doing?
- What are our strongest performing products or services? Why? How can we elevate those?
- What are our weakest performing products or services? Why? How can we minimise or eliminate those?
- Based on the trends, what are our growth expectations? What is the best case/worst case scenario?
- What cost base do we need to service the best case/worst case scenario?
- Where do we need to increase/decrease investment in our cost base?

The answers to these questions will provide necessary insights to set aspirational yet realistic targets on the path towards the 10-year goal.

To get the right qualitative data in the room

What do your people think are your greatest opportunities and challenges?

What do they struggle with and what opportunities do they see? Their insights, generated from real-time experiences with your customers, suppliers, and each other are valuable sources of information that can inform and validate the financial analysis.

To gather their insights and engage them in the process of strategy creation, ask each team leader to facilitate a team SOAR session – inviting teams to contribute to creating the annual strategic vision and plan.

SOAR is positive psychology's answer to the traditional SWOT framework. Instead of analysing **S**trengths, **W**eaknesses, **O**pportunities and **T**hreats, we focus on amplifying the positive by looking at: **S**trengths, **O**pportunities, **A**spirations, **R**esults.

I prefer the SOAR framework because:

- Opportunities and weaknesses are two sides of the same coin and often reveal the same things. Also, people don't like talking about weaknesses; it sounds negative and generates negative emotions which can bring their energy down.

- Aspirations and results give us new data that we don't access from SWOT – aspirations inform the vision and strategic goals of the business; results inform the KPIs we can access to measure success.

Strengths: What can we build on?

Opportunities: What are our stakeholders asking for?

Aspirations: What do we care deeply about?

Results: How do we know we are succeeding?

Questions to prompt SOAR sessions are provided in the table following.

Questions to prompt your SOAR sessions

Strengths: What can we build on?	Opportunities: What are our stakeholders asking for?
What are we most proud of as an organisation? How does that reflect our greatest strength? What makes us unique? What can we be best at in our world? What is our proudest achievement in the last year or two? How do we use our strengths to get results? How do our strengths fit with the realities of the marketplace? What do we do or provide that is world class for our customers, our industry and other potential stakeholders?	How do we make sense of opportunities provided by the external forces and trends? What are the top three opportunities on which we should focus our efforts? How can we best meet the needs of our stakeholders, including customers, employees, shareholders and community? How can we reframe challenges to be seen as existing opportunities? What new skills do we need to move forward?
Aspirations: What do we care deeply about?	Results: How do we know we are succeeding?
When we explore our values and aspirations, what are we deeply passionate about? Reflecting on Strengths and Opportunities conversations, who are we, who should we become and where do we go in the future? What is our most compelling aspiration? What strategic initiatives (e.g. projects, programs, processes) would support our aspirations?	Considering our Strengths, Opportunities and Aspirations: What meaningful measures would indicate that we are on track to achieving our goals? What are three to five indicators that would create a scorecard that addresses a triple bottom line of profit, people and planet? What resources are needed to implement vital projects? What are the best rewards to support those who achieve our goals?

Collate team SOAR responses and combine themes into a single SOAR card that you can present at the strategy workshop.

THE ANNUAL STRATEGY RETREAT

Once you have done the pre-work, the next step is to plan the content and activities you will cover during your strategy retreat. It's important to get this right to achieve maximum bang-for-buck for your time together. Careful planning also ensures your people feel their time is valued.

Set the scene

Set the scene by describing the objectives for the retreat and running through the agenda. Invite everyone to share their personal objectives for the time together. Ensure everyone's objectives are captured and mention how and where each objective will be addressed. If there are objectives for which there is no clear space in the agenda – capture these on a parking lot and agree to get to them if you can find the time.

Review performance of previous 12 months and take stock of the market

This is an important session in which you objectively assess your performance over the last 12 months. Talk through the results of the pre-work, sharing the quantitative financial analysis and qualitative SOAR analysis. Report on achievements against your last Business Plan (if you had one) and identify any priorities that are yet to complete and must be carried over into the next 12 months.

> Congratulate and celebrate successes and wins from the year that was.

Revisit purpose and values

Once they are set, your purpose and values rarely change. In *Good to Great* Jim Collins talks about enduring companies who recognise the importance of preserving their core values and purpose while ensuring that their business strategies and operating practices endlessly adapt to a changing world. Check in with the group on whether you all feel the purpose and values statements still adequately reflect who you are as an organisation, and workshop the feedback if there are ways to sharpen them up.

If you have a Culture Plan, this would be a good time to report on the success of the plan against the culture goals and targets; including any insights from engagement survey results if you've run one. If your Culture Plan needs to be reviewed to address gaps or opportunities; discuss how, when, and who will be involved in contributing to renewing the initiatives that drive a more positive workplace experience for the company.

Reset your one-page Business Plan

If you have effectively reviewed performance and revisited your purpose and values, the rest of the retreat will be a straightforward process of workshopping your new one-year and three-year growth targets on the path to your 10-year vision; agreeing on your strategic pillars (are they the same or do they change); and the goals, KPIs and priorities for each pillar.

Continue to draw on the data from the pre-work as most of your answers to these questions will have already been provided through the analysis. What you need is agreement and consensus from the group – the people who are going to be responsible for achieving these goals and KPIs. The main focus for these sessions is to facilitate open conversations, listening to all viewpoints and extracting the simple truths that everyone is willing to agree on.

Key questions to explore are:

- What are our new one-year and three-year goals on the path to our 10-year vision?

- What are our pillars of success?

- What are our goals and KPIs for each of these pillars?

- What are the priorities that give us the best chances of achieving our KPIs?

- Who leads which project and how will that person track and report on it?

Invest time in team building and leadership development

If you have organised a two-day retreat, create space in your agenda for team building and leadership development exercises that develop the capacity of your leaders for self-awareness, self-leadership and inspiring high performance.

Focus on developing any one of the three leadership behaviours outlined in part II of this book, including their capacity to:

- set standards

- normalise feedback

- coach strengths.

The feedback rounding exercise mentioned in chapter 8 is a great way to bond the team and sharpen up their skills of giving and receiving feedback.

Wrap up

There are a few key points to successfully close your retreat:

- Revisit the individual objectives shared at the start and address any items that have not yet been discussed.

- Ask everyone to self-reflect and provide feedback on the workshop itself – what worked well, and what could you all have done better? By doing this each time, you will continuously improve your workshop process.

- Agree on the next steps to finalising and signing off on the plan. Identify who will draft the document and how it will be approved internally. Perhaps it needs to be reviewed and approved by a board before it can be communicated and cascaded.

- Confirm the internal launch plan and expectations of who will cascade the plan to teams. It may be that senior leaders of several departments need to team up to foster cross-departmental collaboration.

- Agree on the process to monitor and evaluate progress. How will dashboards and reports be generated? In what forums will you review your results?

COMMUNICATING THE PLAN

Communicating the one-page Business Plan is just as important as the creation of the plan itself. Make your plan visually appealing and on-brand – have it graphically designed incorporating your styles, colours and logos. Share copies of the plan digitally and leverage the talents of your marketing and communications teams to think about engaging ways to communicate it.

Ideally, the plan should be released by the Founder or CEO via a live presentation or recorded video. It is important for the team to see and hear how their leader interprets and talks about strategy. This generates energy, focus and interest among the whole crew.

In addition to presenting the plan, this is a good opportunity to present organisation results from the last 12 months, celebrate wins and share the lessons and insights gained through shared reflections from the senior team to foster organisational learning and adaptation.

A structure to guide the presentation of the annual Business Plan is provided in the following diagram.

Annual plan communication: presentation structure

1. PURPOSE (why, how, what)	2. VALUES	3. COMPANY RESULTS against last 12-month KPIs
4. GREATEST WINS BIGGEST LESSONS	5. VISION 10-year goal New 3-year goal New 1-year goal	6. PILLAR 1 Goals, KPIs and priorities
7. PILLAR 2 Goals, KPIs and priorities	8. PILLAR 3 Goals, KPIs and priorities	9. PILLAR 4 Goals, KPIs and priorities

22

Cascade and align

A well-defined and succinct one-page Business Plan without a process to translate that plan into action is just a good read. Strategic goals, targets and priorities are set by the senior or executive team, but teams and individuals should have a large degree of autonomy over how that work is delivered. The Business Plan is cascaded to a Team Plan and to My Plan via Team Plan workshops and annual performance reviews.

Cascading the Business Plan

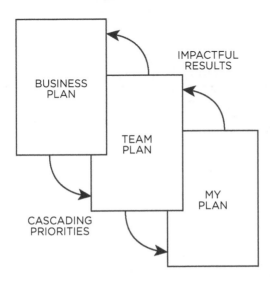

Team Plan

KPIs

TEAM PRIORITIES
Finance
Customer
Process
People

TEAM CULTURE AND LEARNING GOALS

My Plan

KPIs

MY PRIORITIES

Finance

Customer

Process

People

DEVELOPMENT GOALS

Professional
Health/wellbeing
Career

THE TEAM PLAN

Team Plans are created in annual workshops following the release of the annual Business Plan and are an essential accountability for senior managers to initiate and lead. Every single team in your organisation from frontline customer-facing to warehouse teams should participate.

These important communication forums help teams understand their role and contribution in delivering the Business Plan and map out their approach to delivering strategic objectives.

The Team Plan includes all the KPIs and priorities for which that department is responsible that appear on the front and back pages of the Business Plan. In addition, they include sub-KPIs or sub-priorities that are more specific to that team.

The Team Plan may also include a section on the team culture and learning goals. For example; there may be initiatives from the Culture Plan (if you have one) that the team need to engage in or contribute to. In addition, there may be shared skill sets that the team need training in together – such as programs aimed at developing self-leadership, emotional intelligence or resilience capabilities; or technical skills relevant to their work area.

The Team Plan is an essential tool to engage new team members.

Covering off on the existing Team Plan should be part of every new team member's induction.

Like the Business Plan, the Team Plan may be a simple one-page plan but may also include more detailed plans mapping out the stages and timelines for new initiatives and projects.

Team Plan workshops

Team Plan workshops mimic Business Plan workshops, with one key point of difference: they provide teams with the opportunity to deep dive into the detail and planning required to implement priorities for which they are responsible or contribute to.

Annual Team Plan workshops allow teams to assess performance, celebrate successes, identify lessons learned, and reset their goals for the next 12 months. This process provides individuals with clarity on how they each contribute to team and organisational results.

A basic structure for an annual Team Plan workshop is:

- revisit purpose, values and vision

- assess the team's performance from last 12 months

- celebrate wins and identify lessons learned

- build the Team Plan for the next 12 months – capturing all the priorities for which your team has a delegated priority on the back page of the Business Plan, and expanding these to their sub-priorities

- identify owners for each priority

- identify any team culture and learning goals and leveraging options from your Culture Plan (if you have one) that can be planned for and met in future team sessions

- create a list of actionables for the quarter ahead.

Quarterly Team Plan workshops provide regular checkpoints for teams to:

- **Reflect** on the numbers and assess performance relative to expectations.

- **Reset** goals, KPIs and team structures in order to remain agile and adaptive.

- **Reprioritise** and realign on actionables for the following quarter.

Quarterly Team Plan workshops provide opportunities to re-establish the team structure, highlighting any changes to roles that have occurred in the review period, incorporating new team members and empowering individuals with clarity and accountability for their own performance. They are also opportunities for training or development in new processes or systems that build team capacity.

A basic structure for a quarterly Team Plan workshop is:

- Revisit purpose, values and vision.

- Review your team KPIs, dashboards and assess team's results.

- Celebrate achievements for the quarter.

- Identify focus areas for the quarter ahead.

- Work through specific challenges or opportunities as required.

- Present the team structure, highlighting any changes to role accountabilities.

MY PLAN

The individual outcome of the cascading process is a dedicated performance and development plan that clearly outlines individual goals and KPIs derived from the Team Plan. For new starters, these are probationary goals. For all other team members, these are annual goals, revisited on a quarterly basis.

> **My Plans are created in partnership between the team member and their manager and should encompass a broader and more holistic perspective than just a set of KPIs and performance priorities.**

They should also incorporate that individual's learning goals, wellbeing goals and career goals. Employees are motivated by more than financial gain; many are driven by the prospect of advancing their skills and knowledge in pursuit of a more fulfilling career, and to pair this with work–life balance that meets their needs. Every person's situation is unique, and their circumstances evolve over time as their lives and family commitments change. An individual's plan is a place to consider these mitigating factors and create a balance of goals that will enable that individual to work at their performance edge.

Each KPI in your Team Plan should be attributable to an individual in your team. In *Traction*, Gino Wickman says that every role has a number. This gives each role total clarity on how they impact performance.

There are great-quality online performance and development platforms emerging that enable managers and their teams to capture all performance data online. These platforms are a fantastic way to securely store performance data and enable real-time reporting. They can, however, require a significant time and money investment to be successfully implemented and fully leveraged by all people leaders and their teams.

In the absence of online performance tools, design a simple template that individuals and teams use to have performance conversations. At a minimum, the template should include an individual's KPIs, performance priorities and development goals.

My Plans are created in annual performance reviews and revisited in regular one-on-ones. In the next chapter, we'll look at some strategies for conducting these effectively.

Cascading Business Plans to Team Plans and My Plans is a constantly evolving process of creating alignment by getting strategy out of people's heads and into something actionable. These processes embed the skills for people to set meaningful goals that are relevant to the business. Business Plans inform everyone in the business what success looks like. Team Plans and My Plans empower employees with the opportunities to map the path to success in ways that are both meaningful and motivating.

23

Evaluate and review

Fostering a culture of openness and transparency means regularly evaluating and reviewing performance. People leaders provide clarity and alignment by setting goals and KPIs during performance reviews and Team Plan workshops. These are revisited in regular forums to evaluate progress, celebrate wins and reflect on lessons learned along the way.

Regular evaluation and review forums create context, meaning and connection to your company's purpose, values and vision. They create a cadence around which all work activities revolve and help teams remain not just accountable, but motivated, because they are times when we actively observe progress and experience a sense of achievement.

> **The more connected your team are to the purpose, values, vision, strategy and culture, the more they are empowered to contribute.**

While cascading and alignment happens from the top down, measurement and reporting happens from the bottom up. Performance is measured and reflected upon in annual performance reviews, performance check-ins, team monthly dashboard reports, and quarterly CEO updates.

Let's have a look at each of these.

ANNUAL PERFORMANCE REVIEWS

The single biggest opportunity a team member has to discuss their career or personal development, working environment, engagement or contentment levels is their performance review. Having a regular review period that follows the release of an annual Business Plan allows you to achieve three things:

1. Review individual achievements against My Plan.
2. Set KPIs and priorities for the next 12 months.
3. Revisit job descriptions to ensure they are relevant.

Together, job descriptions and individual performance plans provide clarity and significance to every role within your business and allow you to maximise team strengths and capabilities.

PERFORMANCE CHECK-INS

While annual performance reviews are important for setting annual performance and development goals, many leaders make the mistake of adopting a 'set and forget' mindset once the review period is complete. Performance check-ins are a way to systematise performance, development and behaviour conversations (described in chapter 10). Ensure they happen at a minimum on a quarterly basis (following Team Plan workshops) or even more regularly like monthly or bi-monthly.

> Performance check-ins are coaching conversations between leaders and their teams to provide an important accountability and support mechanism in ultimately delivering results.

At a performance check-in the team member and their people leader assess the degree to which they are meeting their KPIs, and identify the habits or actions to focus on between check-ins.

A simple numbering system can be adopted to provide an objective way of assessing whether the team member is meeting standards. For example:

- 1 = Exceeding: outperforming their KPIs

- 2 = Meeting: meeting their KPIs

- 3 = Still learning: acquiring the skills necessary to translate efforts into results

- 4 = Not meeting: consistently underperforming

Unless individuals have visibility on their results and an opportunity for constructive feedback, they are not enabled to improve performance. Implementing a regular feedback and accountability loop drives high performance by identifying the behaviours, actions and habits that drive results.

TEAM MONTHLY DASHBOARD REPORTS

The team monthly dashboard report is a simple report that is built from the ground up and leveraged to assess performance of each team or department. Reports from all departments can be combined to generate a monthly executive report that is reviewed and discussed at management and/or board level.

When I was working as the in-house performance partner at Swisse Wellness, it was strategically and ethically important to us to consistently achieve engagement scores of greater than 85% and be recognised in Australia as an Employer of Choice.

To achieve those outcomes, we were allocated 7% of total company revenue to invest in people, including salaries, benefits and all other people-related costs like recruitment, training, and health and wellness programs such as a fully stocked kitchen to feed the team healthy breakfasts and lunches.

As a People and Culture (P&C) team – we each had responsibility for managing these different 'cost centres', but more importantly, we created a monthly People & Culture report to which we'd each contribute one or two slides. As the Performance Partner, I reported on:

- engagement and climate survey data

- progress on engagement projects

- team completion of six-monthly performance reviews

- training delivery, attendance and evaluation.

Other P&C team members reported on safety measures; recruitment, induction and onboarding measures; leave and turnover measures; take up of benefits; health, wellness and social inclusion opportunities; and participation in our volunteering programs.

Each month we'd review our results with our P&C Director as a team before she completed her executive summary and submitted the deck to the CEO's EA to be included in the monthly board pack.

Those meetings with our P&C director were essential moments in our month to celebrate our wins, observe trends, and seek opportunities for continuous improvement. They were visibility sessions, and while we shared team wins and challenges, we assumed individual accountability for our KPIs.

THE CEO UPDATE

The CEO update is the leader's chance to report company-wide results and inform the whole team on how the organisation is tracking against the Business Plan. It is also her or his opportunity to identify focus areas for the next quarter, maintaining collective attention on strategic priorities. This organisation-level feedback mechanism serves a number of important purposes:

- It educates the team on the business of running a business – it helps all staff understand the relevance and meaning of terms like revenue, margin, brand awareness and Net Promoter Score.

- It gets people focused on performance by highlighting the actions and behaviours that impact results.

- It allows the team to recalibrate and realign their priorities based on the shifting nature of the business or market. By highlighting where teams need to focus for the next quarter, the CEO directs team alignment on projects and priorities that are meaningful and relevant to the business as a whole.

Business Plan quarterly update presentation structure

1. PURPOSE (why, how, what)	2. VALUES	3. VISION 10-year goal 3-year goal 1-year goal	4. COMPANY KPI DASHBOARD
5. PILLAR 1 PRIORITIES Q1 achievements Q2 focus areas	6. PILLAR 2 PRIORITIES Q1 achievements Q2 focus areas	7. PILLAR 3 PRIORITIES Q1 achievements Q2 focus areas	8. PILLAR 4 PRIORITIES Q1 achievements Q2 focus areas

WORK-IN-PROGRESS MEETINGS (WIPS)

Work-in-progress or WIP meetings are regular one-on-one meetings between team members and their managers. These are important times for individuals to progress decision making on their priorities, gain valuable coaching and feedback, and share insights on the operating context. Ideally, these are weekly or at the very least fortnightly. Team members should set their own agenda for these meetings, coming prepared with issues for discussion and sign off so they may effectively progress their workloads.

Weekly WIP meetings:

- provide individual team members with predictable access to their key decision maker – they don't need to fight or 'beg' for time

- create a discipline around saving your items up for the weekly WIP, minimising ad hoc emails and conversations that are not urgent

- encourage teams to be structured and planned, getting the most value out of their time with their manager

- drive accountability – individuals are more motivated to achieve action items from the last meeting rather than turning up with no progress to report

- foster relationships of trust and respect because managers make time to coach and support their people.

Regular evaluation and review forums create context, meaning and connection to your company's vision and mission. They create a cadence around which all work activities revolve and help keep people not just accountable, but motivated, because they are the moments where progress and achievement are recognised.

> **By implementing regular evaluation and review forums, leaders create a failsafe for strategy execution, constantly realigning effort towards shared objectives.**

The table below summarises the cadence of meeting rhythms that support the full strategy creation to strategy execution process.

Annual forums	Quarterly forums	Monthly forums	Weekly forums
Annual strategy retreat	CEO Business Plan update	Performance check-ins	Team WIPs
			Individual WIPs
Performance reviews	Team Plan workshops	Team dashboard reports	

24

Where strategy often goes wrong

There are three main reasons why organisations fail to extract full value from their strategy creation to strategy execution process:

1. We fail to align on a single source of the truth.
2. We don't place enough emphasis on strategy execution.
3. We get lost in translation.

WE FAIL TO ALIGN ON A SINGLE SOURCE OF THE TRUTH

A large part of strategy creation is the facilitation of the coming together of multiple viewpoints. It's about finding common ground, testing that we are all talking about the same thing, and agreeing on how we are going to work together to get there.

A CEO I once worked with was a visionary, an exceptional strategist and clear communicator. He would have a new idea. He would communicate that idea in meetings and town hall sessions. His executive team would take what they heard and translate his ideas into their Strategic Plan for their part of the business.

The challenge was that each executive would execute *their* version of his story. His truth was reinterpreted through their truth, and so multiple variations of the truth were executed. Unintentionally, misalignment occurred.. The outcome: wasted effort and slower growth.

If a strategy stays in someone's head — if it's not physically put down on paper and confirmed among all those who must contribute — then it is subject to misinterpretation and will lead to misalignment. Oftentimes, we think we've communicated when we've had a conversation. But most times, we forget that each individual is going to receive that information through their own filter.

Entrepreneurial leaders are visionaries. They are ideators. They think up new ideas regularly and want to see them implemented fast. The challenge is that they are often three steps ahead of everyone else. While the rest of the team are scrambling to keep up with the last priority, their visionary leader has moved on and is keen to translate the next opportunity.

Where many fast-growing or fast-moving teams fail is in not having a strategy creation process that translates ideas into a shared written form that is easy to produce, to understand and to communicate. We need to remain agile, but not at the expense of alignment.

WE DON'T PLACE ENOUGH EMPHASIS ON STRATEGY EXECUTION

As a consultant who facilitates annual strategy and planning sessions, I get to see a great deal of energy and effort go into the creation and communication of the big-picture organisational strategy. I reconnected with one such group eight months after their annual strategy event. While our goal for this follow-up session was to build leadership and communication skills rather than revisiting their strategy, we inevitably discussed their success at executing their plan.

When I asked how it was going, there was a pause. Then one chap declared, 'it's dead in the water!'

After much discussion (was it or wasn't it dead in the water?), we sought to take the lessons and insights from their experience, rather than point fingers of blame.

Interestingly, in assessing the detail, they were surprised to find that they had actually realised about 50% of what was on the plan. Perhaps that was luck? Chance? Or had it actually permeated their minds and started organising their behaviour without conscious effort? What they lacked was not a good plan, but the discipline and process around strategy execution.

They came to a place of reckoning that their plan was:

- too ambitious – they'd bitten off more than they could chew

- not talked about (at all) in executive team meetings

- not talked about (very little) in one-on-ones with teams

- therefore not actually being lived or breathed in the organisation, and potentially damaging their reputation as executives and leaders of the business.

Strategy creation without strategy execution is just wasted effort. According to the *Harvard Business Review*, companies realise only 40% to 60% of their strategies' potential value.

Whatever the outcome, for that group the plan was deemed to have a pulse and, if well managed, would help them realise latent potential in their business. They agreed their remedy to strategy execution success was threefold:

1. Get much sharper with their goals – less is more.

2. Create simple dashboards that inform progress against key KPIs.

3. Talk about it systematically – in teams, in one-on-ones, in executive monthly meetings, in their own heads.

Thinking that your job is done after releasing your Strategic Plan is like giving up after two kilometres of a 42-kilometre marathon ... you have barely even started.

Jeroen De Flander, author of *Strategy Execution Heroes*, talks about **strategy tourists**. These are people who:

- love big words to make themselves sound more important

- are more interested in looking good, than being good

- delegate all the strategy execution work to consultants

- restart a new strategy process every year

- are somewhat lazy.

De Flander encourages us to be strategy heroes rather than strategy tourists.

> Put as much effort into your strategy execution process as you do into your strategy creation process and you will realise 90%-plus of the results you anticipate in your plan.

WE GET LOST IN TRANSLATION

Jeroen De Flander talks about 'initiative management' as the point where organisational performance meets individual performance. Initiative management is where the rubber meets the road; where people are connected to strategy. His research published in *The Strategy Execution Research Report* (2009) indicates that initiative management is the weakest link in the strategy execution chain. The research conducted with 1100 organisations of varying sizes from across the globe indicates that 27% believe strategic initiatives aren't being managed correctly, with the four main reasons being:

- 37% resource initiatives poorly

- 34% budget inadequately

- 26% fail to create clear ownership

- 21% launch the wrong projects.

In addition, De Flander's research reported that:

- 30% receive no information on how to execute strategy

- 24% receive no useful strategy information from other departments

- 18% are unable to explain how to set individual objectives

- 13% are unable to explain the strategy.

There is often a big chasm between an overarching organisational strategy and an individual's understanding of their role in achieving that strategy. Initiative management is the act of translation. It is the work that leaders must do to decipher big-picture strategy into individual opportunity. For example; most Strategic Plans will have a finance target aimed at saving costs, such as a cost of goods (COGS) target. A COGS target of 19% is not going to mean much to the average person who has never run a business or completed a business degree. Nor should it. The average employee is not a business administrator. But a conversation at team level about how that particular team can help the business save on costs by minimising waste or improving productivity means something more tangible.

Delegating a COGS target is a passive exercise. Facilitating a conversation with a team about finding smarter ways of working is an active and engaging exercise.

> **Leaders at every level need to communicate strategy and facilitate conversations where people are enabled to make meaning of their role in achieving organisational objectives.**

These conversations need to happen top down, so that leaders first understand their role before facilitating understanding for their teams.

Strategy creation is not a passive delegation process. It is an **active participation** process that happens at every level in an organisation in order to breed success for every individual.

Part IV summary

- Strategy is enhanced when it is treated as a dynamic process of creation followed by execution.

- The balance of time is about 20% strategy creation, 80% strategy execution. Each time we take a swing at strategy creation we reflect on our learned experience, reset our approach and reprioritise our actions.

- In an open-systems view, strategy is a representation of the way links are made between the inside and the outside of the organisation, and between its various sub-components.

- The key to realising the full value from your strategy and gaining alignment across a whole organisation is to get it out of people's heads and onto a page to make it not just clear, but also actionable.

- The Strategy System is your process for strategy creation and execution that ensures your organisation remains adaptive and responsive in your chosen market.

- The Strategy System aligns the whole team to work collaboratively. It involves:

  a. creating a one-page Business Plan that is clear and actionable

  b. cascading KPIs through to teams and individuals through strategy creation workshops

  c. regular review forums to stay connected and aligned to the results and progress towards achieving your company mission.

- One-page Business Plans get everyone on the same page. They translate vision into clear and measurable action:

  – The front page of the plan details the purpose, values, vision, pillars, goals and KPIs.

- The back page of the plan details the priorities to achieve goals and KPIs, departments contributing, and the leaders responsible.

- Creating a one-page Business Plan is a team engagement exercise that is best performed on an annual strategy retreat with the senior team. A well-run retreat results in alignment of vision, clarity of direction and accountability of leadership.

- The one-page Business Plan is cascaded to a Team Plan and to My Plan via Team Plan workshops and annual performance reviews. These communication forums give every individual the opportunity to contribute to, and have ownership over, the strategy creation process.

- Fostering a culture of openness and transparency means regularly evaluating and reviewing performance. Performance is measured and reflected upon in performance check-ins, team monthly reporting sessions, quarterly CEO updates, and regular Work-In-Progress (WIP) meetings.

- Strategy goes wrong when organisations:
  - fail to align on a single source of the truth
  - don't place enough emphasis on strategy execution
  - get lost in translation.

- An actionable strategy is one on which teams fully align, focus on achieving and are empowered to implement.

Bringing it all together

When we bring together the systems for leadership, culture and strategy, we see a mega-ladder of high performance where all systems are interconnected. This is where we see the high-performance system producing remarkable results.

The High-Performance Ladder

THE REALITY				THE RESULT		
Organisational system	Leadership	Culture	Strategy	Focus	Effort	Market performance
Integrated	Inspiring	Adaptive	Actionable	Continuous improvement	Amplified	x 10
Coherent	Supportive	Inclusive	Clear	Task performance	Sustained	x 5
Connected	Directive	Siloed	Complicated	Task completion	Applied	x 1
Disjointed	Busy	Defensive	Outdated	Internal competition	Scattered	x -1
Disconnected	Hostile	Toxic	Invisible	Self-protection	Withheld	x -5

Adopting the systems for leadership, culture and strategy described in this book will elevate your:

- leaders from being hostile to inspiring
- culture from being toxic to adaptive
- strategy from being invisible to actionable.

This will result in people who focus on continuous improvement, amplifying their efforts and delivering superior market performance compared to competitors.

WHERE DO I START?

Hopefully by now you're convinced of the need for systems of performance.

So, the only question that remains now is, where do you start?

Do you start with the ...

- System for Leadership
- System for Culture, or
- System for Strategy?

Are all equally important. These are concepts that cross every organisational boundary. They are relevant and meaningful in every team, at every level, at all stages of business development.

| Chances are you are not starting with a blank canvas.

More than likely you have a business or a team who have been operating at full speed for a while now and the cracks are starting to show. If you can identify with any of the rungs on those ladders below the top rung, then congratulations – you have the opportunity to realise more potential!

Here's an easy way to diagnose where to start. Place a mark on the high-performance ladders where your organisation currently sits in relation to leadership, culture and strategy. Whatever the lowest rung is – that's where you begin.

For example: if you think leaders in your organisation are typically **busy**, but your culture is **inclusive** and your strategy is **clear** – then start by developing leadership capability.

If you're still at a stalemate and you need more guidance, here's what I recommend:

- Year 1: Start with culture → ignite passion
- Year 2: Move to strategy → define high performance
- Year 3: Develop leadership → connect people to purpose (their own and the company's)

Treat this as a three- to four-year journey of adoption, with each stage representing a focus for the year ahead. Embed what you've created, then introduce something new. Try to do too much, too quickly, and you'll fail to realise the full value of your efforts. This as a continuous improvement journey with no destination.

Year 1

Define your purpose and values. Get clear on the business's *why*, *how* and *what*. Know how you create shared value amongst your stakeholders. Ensure that it is authentic and real – it's not something you're doing because this book says so. Do it because you want to – it aligns with your personal purpose and vision for a fulfilled life.

If you don't know what your personal purpose and vision is – engage a coach and define it. If you are a business leader, CEO or founder – make yourself easy to follow by having a mission and values that others can actually buy into. Don't leave it up to your dynamic personality to inspire your followers and employees. This wears thin after a while. Get clear on how achieving the business purpose is personally fulfilling and motivating to you. Running a business takes enormous energy and effort – there are lots of ups and downs. The only way to stay motivated is to tap into what intrinsically drives you and connects you to the organisation's mission.

Develop your Culture Plan. Get real on living your values at every touchpoint in the employee experience. Live your values inside out and build passion for your cause. Focus on building an incredible customer and employee experience. Start measuring customer satisfaction and employee engagement. Set yourself realistic targets to step towards becoming a recognised employer of choice. Communicate internally and externally how your Culture Plan sets you apart from your competitors to attract and maintain talented and passionate people who will drive your business further, faster. Take Jim Collins's advice and get the right people in the right seats on the bus, before you decide where to drive it.

Year 2

Strategy creation. Define your strategy. How are you going to win in the market you've chosen? Where do you need to invest ? Where do you need to innovate? To adapt? To evolve? Get clear on what high performance looks like, how you will measure it and what projects you'll align the team on to deliver it. Engage with your senior team to do this – organise a retreat and bond together as a group. Spend what you can given your financial performance. If you've had a good year – treat the team to something special. If you're strapped for cash – ask your dad if you can use his pool room. Don't let money be a barrier. Time together is more important than a fancy venue. If you're restricted by geography, travel limitations or social distancing restrictions, design an engaging online experience and think of ways to recreate a retreat-like experience – send the team care packs; do a yoga/meditation class online together; have a trivia night or social element.

Strategy execution. Develop a quarterly operating rhythm of strategy creation, cascade, and review. Align team and individual goals and KPIs to the Business Plan. Get everyone used to being accountable to a number (and not just revenue). Celebrate the high performers who also demonstrate positive behaviour and hold them up as role models. Support those who are struggling with targeted coaching and development plans that leverage strengths, and manage out people who are no longer a good fit either for their skills or their behaviours.

Year 3

Develop leadership capability. Develop the skills of your leaders to inspire high performance and coach your people towards achieving stretch goals and targets. Recognise that leadership itself is a learned skill and one that requires training, feedback and coaching to master. Start measuring strengths and adopt a strengths-based mentality – asking leaders and teams to appreciate and recognise how diversity of strengths and skill sets adds value to the group.

Make leaders accountable to demonstrating the company values and achieving Business Plans. Implement 360-degree feedback using a validated and reliable psychometric tool to raise leaders' self-awareness and improve their self-management with coaching. Add KPIs for all leaders that their people all have performance and development goals; that they conduct quarterly team planning workshops and annual reviews; and that they deliver a team engagement score greater than 75%.

Engage your people and culture specialists (inhouse or externals) to develop internal training programs, policies and processes so that every new manager who joins will be trained in how to create strategy, demonstrate leadership and reinforce the culture through every stage of the employee lifecycle. Embed your system within the frameworks of how you operate, particularly at induction of new leaders in the business.

THE BALANCE OF TIME

We all know how important it is for leaders to work *on* the business, not *in* the business.

> **Working on the business means implementing and integrating the systems for leadership, culture and strategy.**

It means getting these systems working together; like a fidget spinner that sustains its own momentum.

So how much time should leaders spend working on implementing and integrating systems of performance?

The answer depends on the level of leadership responsibility you hold. All employees, regardless of seniority, are leaders. Those who are not responsible for a team are still responsible for themselves, contribute to the culture, and play a part in the creation and execution of strategy. But those in more senior positions – founders, CEOs, executives, and senior leaders – have more responsibility and therefore greater influence on performance.

A simple way to consider the balance of time is to consider your *leading* vs *doing* ratio.

Leading versus doing ratio

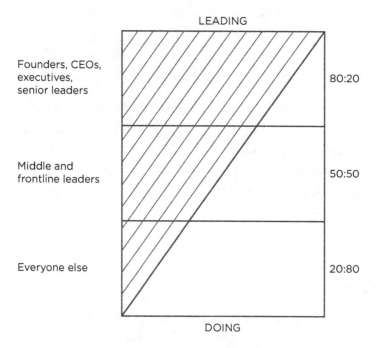

In this diagram, **leading** is time given to implementing systems of performance for leadership, culture and strategy (time 'on' the business).

Doing is completing tasks that require technical knowledge or specialist expertise relevant to your role (time 'in' the business).

The more senior you are, the more responsibility you have for the performance of others and the more time you should be leading rather than doing. That is:

- Founders, CEOs, executives and senior leaders should aim for an 80/20 balance; 80% leading or 'on' the business; 20% doing or 'in' the business.

- Middle managers or frontline leaders should aim for a 50/50 balance; 50% leading, 50% doing.

- All others not in people leadership positions should allocate a 20/80 balance of time: 20% leading, 80% doing.

This means that, if you're a senior leader, to truly drive a high-performance environment, a successful day is one spent largely in front of people. When you lead more and do less, you are effectively enabling others to learn, grow, improve and deliver their accountabilities. This is the fastest way to progress every role towards greater capacity and complexity. This is the only way to bring everyone closer to their performance edge.

This also means that if you enjoy *doing* the work, then don't work yourself out of a strength by taking on greater leadership responsibility. Stay in your strength zone. If you're a Founder whose passion and energy is all for the product or service you deliver, then bring on board a partner or CEO who is strong in leading, communicating and implementing systems and processes and allows you to focus on doing what you do best.

When leading – the work happens in meetings. Not in between. Leaders who effectively transition from 'doing' to 'leading' embrace this idea and gain enormous energy from seeing their people thrive and meet their performance edge.

To lead is to release control and accept that your job *is* implementing systems of performance. Your teams' success is your success.

OVER TO YOU

Remember: purpose, passion and performance drive profit. Each time the wheel turns, it gains momentum. Each time you generate shared value for your stakeholders, you are able to invest more money, time and energy back into the system; growing and continually improving it and creating a perpetual cycle of positive exchange.

Purpose, passion and performance drive profit

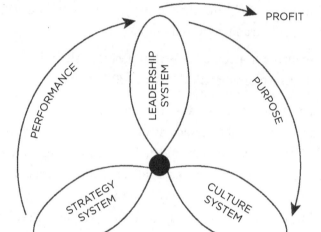

Focusing on your systems for performance generates outstanding results. Systems drive habits which drive results. Herein lies the paradox. Raj Sisoda calls this the Zen-like paradox:

> *Trying harder to make money leads to making less money. To put it another way, the most profit-oriented companies are usually not the most profitable, whereas most companies that are highly profitable are not primarily focused on profit making.*

If we focus on watching the scoreboard, we are taking our eyes off the game. High-performing organisations are less interested in the score, and more interested in perfecting and executing game play.

To generate purpose, passion and performance, focus on the systems for leadership, culture and strategy – and the results will take care of themselves.

Acknowledgements

The only way I've felt truly validated to share these stories and experiences is because I've been lucky enough to work in places with exceptional leaders who created the contexts in which people were inspired to sustain extraordinary standards of performance. I know it's possible not just because I've studied it, but because I've lived it.

Tim Orton at Nous Group was one such leader and is still the benchmark against whom I compare all others. With Tim at the helm, Nous leads the way in flexible workplaces based on trust and respect. At Nous, I thrived. Thank you to all Nous colleagues from that time, and in particular to my Leadership practice colleagues: Lea Thorpe, Christine Wilson, Kim Boekeman, Tim Pence, Jill Tullock, Penelope Cottrill, Julia Cummins, Georgia Murch, Georgia Russell and Christie Allison.

Radek Sali at Swisse Wellness is in the same class of exceptional leaders. His energy, positivity and enthusiasm is infectious! Thank you Radek for writing the foreword to this book – just one of many ways you've supported my journey over the years. Your work continues to inspire us all to lift our game in the service of higher purpose. Helen was right – you truly are the original Light Warrior.

Equally – thank you Catherine Crowley. I was introduced to Catherine at a hens-day lunch hosted by our mutual (and awesomely talented) friend Claire Karafillis (thank you Claire!) and we spent the whole lunch talking about organisational values. We just clicked. The decision to leave Nous Group was not an easy one; but the opportunity to work with Catherine and be part of one of Australia's #1 brands was too good to pass up. Thank you Catherine for being my friend, mentor, and thought partner. You deserve to be credited and recognised for the systems of performance described in this book – we designed and tested these together. And we had *so much fun* doing it. I admire you still and am forever grateful. Having a boss like you is a once in a lifetime thing.

Thank you to my clients who have supported me since starting my own practice. Steve Kloss in particular – you have been unwavering in your commitment to our process and in your advocacy for me within YPO circles. Your ongoing support and endorsement is truly appreciated. There are too many clients to personally thank here but please know I value and learn from every one of you. You are my teachers.

Jamie Cook, Brad Sewell and Radek (again) – thank you for agreeing to be interviewed as part of the research for this book and allowing me to share your stories.

Grant Moffit – thank you for helping my family on our transition to Byron life and generously contributing your time both as a mentor and friend. Clinton and I feel lucky to call you and Natalie our friends.

Thank you Brooke Lyons for your exceptional developmental editing, encouragement and mini coaching sessions! You helped get this thing done. Thank you Michael Hanrahan for your rapid turnaround times and the team at Publish Central for all you do to support self-published authors.

Georgia Murch – you believed in me at Nous and you believe in me now. You keep popping back into my life like a little success fairy – presenting me with opportunities that I can't resist! Thank you for your mentorship and friendship. You're seriously smart and seriously fun. Thank you also for introducing me to the Thought Leader Business School community – the place I now call my professional home.

My work would not be possible without the unbelievable support I have from my family. Thank you to my boys Byron and Lawson, for letting me travel and work for days at a time, never complaining about it. You're two exceptional humans – I am, so, so proud of you. To my support team – Mum, Mahi and Annie – you love and care for our boys and gave your time generously for many years while they were young allowing me to work and study. I literally could not have come to this place without all of you. Dad – thank you for always supporting me and encouraging me to just do what I love. Thank you to all my family members – again too many to mention here but please know you all hold a special place in my heart.

Thank you Christian, Emma-Rose and Auntie Mal for allowing me to share Nick's story. His legacy continues.

Finally, thank you to my husband, Clinton. You are an exceptional leader in your own right. You give generously to our community, and I never stop marvelling at your capacity for empathy and kindness. You are my rock. Thank you for believing in me, encouraging me, forgiving me when I lose myself. We promised to let each other wake up and be whatever we wanted to be every day. Thank you for letting me choose to be an author too. I love you always.

About Stephanie

Stephanie Bown is a performance curator, skilled in enhancing business performance by activating the potential of individuals, teams and organisations.

Stephanie uses an evidence-based approach to embed performance cultures in businesses. Throughout her journey her approach has yielded billion-dollar sales, double-digit growth, and happier and healthier places of work. She has worked with start-ups, SMEs and global powerhouses – and her motivation is always the same: to help people move from simply functioning to fully flourishing.

Stephanie is obsessed with performance; since she was in her early teens Stephanie has studied the deep inner workings of the mind and how people survive or thrive at work. Stephanie grew up in Melbourne, Australia, the youngest of four children. Her early tertiary studies saw her working at Swinburne University's Neuroscience laboratory.

Having completed over nine years of tertiary education and over five professional accreditations, Stephanie has devoted her life to discovering the dynamics of individuals, teams and organisations at work, and lives to share her insights with her clients. Her mission is to deliver life-changing learning experiences.

With a Masters in Organisation Dynamics, Stephanie has a personal and professional interest in group psychodynamics, neuropsychology and behavioural science. She views performance as the intersection between strategy, leadership and culture, and seeks to explore these in parallel, revealing an organisation's performance edge.

A 2600-kilometre bicycle adventure with her now husband through Morocco and Spain in 2002–03 gave time for reflection, followed by a stint in London which included time at global consulting house PwC.

On returning to Australia in 2006, Stephanie worked with Nous Group consultants across a range of national projects in leadership and transformational change, before moving to Swisse Wellness as the Inhouse Performance Specialist. At Swisse, Steph worked with the executive team on business strategy and cultural alignment as they navigated rapid growth for an eventual Australian record $1.6 billion sale to Hong Kong–listed Biostime.

In 2015 Stephanie moved her family (husband Clinton, sons Byron and Lawson) to Byron Bay, where she established her own consulting practice workwellgroup (WWG) with her husband. WWG's offering included wellbeing and mindful leadership retreats in Byron Bay, as well as consulting with clients such as The Vue Group, Stone & Wood Brewing Company, Swisse Wellness, The MaDE Group and Pentana Solutions, among others.

Over the next five years Steph's work focused more on systems of performance for leadership, culture and strategy to activate the potential of individuals, teams and organisations. She offers her services as a speaker, mentor, facilitator, trainer and coach. In 2020, Stephanie rebranded her practice as StephanieBown.com to further reflect her personal offering.

Connect with Steph on LinkedIn, sign-up for regular insights from her website or reach out directly on any of these channels:

W: stephaniebown.com
E: contact@stephaniebown.com
L: linkedin.com/in/stephaniebown1/

References

Adams, L. 'Noel Burch's Four Stages of Learning model'. https://www.gordontraining.com/free-workplace-articles/learning-a-new-skill-is-easier-said-than-done/

Aguinis, H. and O'Boyle, E. (2012). 'The Best and The Rest: Revisiting the norm of normality of individual performance'. *Personnel Psychology*, 65(1), 79–119.

Argyris, C. and Schön, D. (1974). *Theory in Practice: Increasing professional effectiveness*. San Francisco: Jossey-Bass.

Atlassian.com. 'What You Should Really Measure in Your Annual Performance Reviews (and Why)'. https://www.atlassian.com/blog/hr-teams/our-performance-reviews-framework. Accessed 9 August 2020.

Australian Government Fair Work Ombudsman. 'Managing Underperformance'. https://www.fairwork.gov.au/how-we-will-help/templates-and-guides/best-practice-guides/managing-underperformance. Accessed 9 August 2020.

Barr, S. (2017). *Prove It!: How to create a high-performance culture and measurable success*. John Wiley & Sons, Australia.

Biswas-Diener, R. and Dean, B. (2007). *Positive Psychology Coaching: Putting the science of happiness to work for your clients*. John Wiley & Sons, US.

Bollas, C. (1987). *The Shadow of the Object: Psychoanalysis of the unthought known*. Taylor and Francis, UK.

Brown, B. (2018). *Dare to Lead: Brave work. Tough conversations. Whole hearts.* Random House, US.

Buckingham, M. and Coffman, C. (1999). *First, Break All the Rules: What the world's greatest managers do differently.* Gallup Press, US.

Chung, F. 'Atlassian ditches "brilliant jerks" in performance review overhaul'. https://www.news.com.au/finance/work/at-work/atlassian-ditches-brilliant-jerks-in-performance-review-overhaul/news-story/82a5e2abba1939f51d68ae81db8f05bd. Accessed 6 August 2020.

Clear, J. (2018). *Atomic Habits: An easy and proven way to build good habits and break bad ones.* Penguin Random House, UK.

Collins, J. (2001). *Good to Great: Why some companies make the leap and others don't.* Random House, US.

Cooperrider, D.L. and Whitney, D. (2005). *Appreciative Inquiry: A positive revolution in change.* Berrett-Koehler, US.

Corporate Leadership Council. (2002). *Building the High Performance Workforce: A quantitative analysis of the effectiveness of performance management strategies.* US.

Csikszentmihalyi, M. (2008). *The Psychology of Optimal Performance.* Harper Collins Publishers, US.

Culture Amp. 'A guide to mapping your employee experience'. https://www.cultureamp.com/resources-a/whitepapers-ebooks/

De Board, R. (1978). The *Psychoanalysis of Organizations: A psychoanalytic approach to behaviour in groups and organizations.* Routledge, US and Canada.

De Flander, J. (2010). *Strategy Execution Heroes: Business strategy implementation and strategic management demystified.* Self-published.

De Flander, J. (Ed. 2009–10). 'The Strategy Execution Research Report'. https://the-performance-factory.be/en/.

Deci, E.L. and Ryan, R.M. (1985). *Intrinsic Motivation and Self-Determination in Human Behavior.* Plenum, US.

Edmonson, A. (2018). *The Fearless Organization: Creating psychological safety in the workplace for learning, innovation and growth.* John Wiley & Sons, US.

Evans, T. 'Employee benefits: Which perks work?' https://www.seek.com.au/employer/hiring-advice/employee-benefits-perks-work.

Ferriss, T. (2009). *The 4-Hour Work Week: Escape 9-5, live anywhere, and join the new rich*, Harmony Books, US.

Fredrickson, B.L. and Losada, M.F. (2005). 'Positive Affect and the Complex Dynamics of Human Flourishing'. *American Psychologist*, 60(7), 678–686.

Fredrickson, B.L. (2013). 'Updated Thinking on Positivity Ratios'. *American Psychologist*, 68(9), 814-822.

Gallup Press (2019). 'Building a High-Development Culture Through Your Employee Engagement Strategy'. Gallup Inc, US.

Gallup Press, (2017). *State of the Global Workplace.* Gallup Inc, US.

Gallwey, T. (1974). *The Inner Game of Tennis.* Random House, US.

Govindji, R. and Linley, P.A. (2007). 'Strengths Use, Self-Concordance and Well-Being: Implications for strengths coaching and coaching psychologists.' *International Coaching Psychology Review.* 2(2).

Great Place to Work. 2019 Edition. '50 Best Places to Work'. http://www.greatplacetowork.com.au.

Harnish, V. (2014). *Scaling Up: How a few companies make it and why the rest don't.* Gazelles Inc. US.

Housman, M. and Minor, D. (2015). 'Toxic Workers: Working Paper 16-057'. Published online. Harvard Business School, US.

Human Synergistics International, 2014. 'Why Culture and Leadership Matter: Proving the people-performance connection'.

Human Synergistics International, 2016. 'Cutting Through the White Noise: What is Culture?' Whitepaper.

Jones, Q., Dunphy, D., Fishman, R., Larne M. and Canter, C. (2011). 'In Great Company: Unlocking the secrets of cultural transformation. Human Synergistics Australia & Human Synergistics, New Zealand.

Kaagan, S.S. (1999). *Leadership Games: Experiential learning for organizational development.* Sage Publications Inc., US.

Kaplan, R.S. and Norton, D.P. (1996). *The Balanced Scorecard: Translating strategy into action.* Harvard Business School Press. US.

Landsberg, M. (1996). *The Tao of Coaching.* Harper Collins, UK.

Linley, P.A., Nielsen, K.M, Wood, A.M. and Biswas-Diener, R. (2010). 'Using Signature Strengths in Pursuit of Goals: Effects on goal progress, need satisfaction, and well-being, and implications for coaching psychologists'. *International Coaching Psychology Review,* Vol 5, Issue 1, pp.6-15.

Loher, J. and Schwartz, T. (2003) *The Power of Full Engagement.* The Free Press, US.

Lombardo, M. and Eichinger, W. (1996). *The Career Architect Development Planner* (1st ed.). Lominger, US.

Losada, M. (1999). 'The Complex Dynamics of High Performance Teams.' *Mathematical and Computer Modelling,* 30(9–10), 179–192.

Losada, M. and Heaphy, E. (2004). 'The Role of Positivity and Connectivity in the Performance of Business Teams'. *American Behavioural Scientist,* 47(6), 740–765.

Mankins, M. and Steele, R. (2005) 'Turning Great Strategy Into Great Performance'. *Harvard Business Review,* July–August 2005.

Miller, E.J. and Rice, A.K. (1967). *Systems of Organisation: The control of task and sentient boundaries.* Tavistock Publications Limited, London. Reprinted in 2001 by Routledge, UK.

Mintzberg, H. 1987, 'Five Ps for Strategy'. *California Management Review,* 30(1), 11–24

Mitchell, S. (2018). *Relentless.* Pan Macmillan, Australia.

Murch, G. (2016). *Fixing Feedback.* John Wiley & Sons, Australia.

Pink, D. (2018). *Drive: The surprising truth about what motivates us.* Canongate Books Ltd, UK.

Prime Minister of Australia Press Statement Transcript. 16 December 2018. < https://www.pm.gov.au/media/press-statement-canberra> Accessed 6 August 2020.

Rice A.K. (1963). *The Enterprise and Its Environment.* Tavistock Publications, UK.

Rice, A.K. (1958). *Productivity and Social Organisations: The Ahmedabad Experiment,* Tavistock Publications, UK.

Sinek, S. 2009. *Start with Why.* Penguin, UK.

Sisodia, R., Sheth, J., Wolfe, D. (2007). *Firms of Endearment: How world-class companies profit from passion and purpose.* Wharton School Publishing, US.

Trist, E.L. and Bamforth, K.W. (1951). 'Some Social and Psychological Consequences of the Longwall Method of Coal-cutting'. *Human Relations.* 4(1): 3–38.

Von Bertalanffy, L. (1969). 'The Theory of Open Systems in Physics and Biology'. In F.E. Emergy (ed.), *Systems Thinking.* Penguin, UK.

Wickman, G. (2011). *Traction: Get a grip on your business.* BenBella Books, US.

Wiseman, L. and McKeown, G. (2010). *Multipliers: How the best leaders make everyone smarter.* Harper Business, US.

World Economic Forum; Centre for the New Economy and Society. The Future of Jobs Report, 2018. http://www3.weforum.org/docs/WEF_Future_of_Jobs_2018.pdf.

Index

CPSIA information can be obtained
at www.ICGtesting.com
Printed in the USA
BVHW042015171021
619165BV00009B/68

9 781922 391704